T0270340

"I know a book is a keeper when the author comes alongside me to point to our shared weaknesses, our silly and self-chosen religious masquerades, and to usher me, with wit and humor and truth, into a life where Jesus is the all-in-all. Matt pulled open my own junk drawer and pointed out all the useless stuff that clutters my soul and centers me on me, then pointed, over and over, to Jesus and his finished work of salvation as God's gift. Not only was the book a sheer joy to read; it centered me on who and what truly matters. By the last page, I loved Jesus more and knew, with profound gratitude, that I am one whom Jesus loves."

Chad Bird
Scholar-in-Residence, 1517

"What a wonderful book! *Junk Drawer Jesus* abounds with inspired imagery and insight about the burdens we accumulate, often without realizing it—and the cluttering effect this can have on our souls. A worldclass communicator, Matt Popovits has given us not only a vital tool for taking spiritual inventory, but a highly readable invitation to faith itself. I loved every chapter."

David Zahl
Author of *Low Anthropology* and *Seculosity*

"In *Junk Drawer Jesus*, Matt Popovits invites us to slow down and examine our religious beliefs as we unpack and rediscover the truth about who Jesus is. This book, full of hope and wisdom, will leave you encouraged as you find rest in the beauty of God's grace."

Tanner Olson
Author and Poet (Writtentospeak.com)

"*Junk Drawer Jesus* could only be written after many years of humble ministry! In it Matt gives us a grace-filled look at our Christian journey, helping us shed the religiosity and idolatry that can weigh us down."

Melanie Penn
Singer/Songwriter

"In today's world, our Faith Life seems less and less like a straight line and more and more like a forest. Branches tangled at every turn, leaves falling everywhere, and the slightest sound or movement causing panic and retreat. Pastor Matt Popovits has a way of writing for those lost in the forest, and making sense of the messiness that is this life. This book will bless those who read it at any time, in any context, and in any age group. Popovits provides us with a gentle reminder of how God is still speaking, and how through the messiness He is still working."

Rev. Dr. Gerard Bolling
Lead Pastor—Bethlehem Lutheran Church in St. Louis, MO
Assistant Professor of Leadership & Theology—Concordia University Texas

"Preaching is a much-maligned word. But, properly understood, preaching delivers a gift: Jesus Christ and His gospel to sinners. In this way, *Junk Drawer Jesus* is preaching at its finest. Popovits powerfully applies Jesus to all kinds of misguided spiritualities that one finds in their theological junk drawer, leaving us with the hope we need in today's typically bleak spiritual landscape. You are going to want to get multiple copies of this one to give to your friends, especially those who are so disenchanted with religion. This book offers something better than what we find in our junk drawers, it preaches Jesus!"

Rev. Bob Hiller
Senior Pastor of Community Lutheran Church in Escondido/San Marcos, CA; content editor for The Craft of Preaching, and co-host of the White Horse Inn podcast.

"Matt Popovits has written a true gift for the church—a modern, instantly accessible Mere Christianity laser-focused on the Gospel written with humor and true insight. Perfect for anyone who wants to examine all the spiritual junk cluttering up their understanding of who Jesus really is and what His message means for them. I have never read a book and wished I had written it as much as Junk Drawer Jesus. This is a perfect gift for someone who is skeptical or dealing with doubt about the Christian faith. I plan on making great use of this book as a small group study in my church. Bravo Matt!"

Frank Hart
Pastor and Author

JUNK DRAWER JESUS

◆

MATT POPOVITS

Foreword by **JARED C. WILSON**

Discarding your
spiritual clutter
& rediscovering the
supremacy of grace

JUNK DRAWER JESUS

MATT POPOVITS
Foreword by **JARED C. WILSON**

Published by:
1517 Publishing
PO Box 54032
Irvine, CA 92619-4032

Publisher's Cataloging-In-Publication Data
(Prepared by Cassidy Cataloguing Services)

Names: Popovits, Matt, author. | Wilson, Jared C., 1975- writer of foreword.
Title: Junk drawer Jesus : discarding your spiritual clutter and rediscovering the
    supremacy of grace / Matt Popovits ; foreword by Jared C. Wilson.
Description: Irvine, CA : 1517 Publishing, [2024] | Includes bibliographical references.
    Identifiers: ISBN: 978-1-956658-48-4 (hardcover) | 978-1-956658-49-1 (paperback) |
    978-1-956658-50-7 (ebook) | 978-1-956658-51-4 (audiobook)
Subjects: LCSH: Spirituality—Christianity. | Christian life. | Jesus Christ—Person
    and offices. | BISAC: RELIGION / Christian Theology / Christology. | RELIGION
    / Christian Theology / General. | RELIGION / Christian Living / General.
Classification: LCC: BV4501.3 .P66 2024 | DDC: 248.4—dc23

Printed in the United States of America.
Cover art by Zachariah James Stuef.

For Ava and Jack.

May the answer always be Jesus.

Give me a piece of the true cross
I long for something Holy
This subculture ain't real

ATOMIC OPERA, "JESUS JUNK"

Table of Contents

Foreword

ONCE I WAS IN A TAXI CAB in Minneapolis, Minnesota, trying to tell the Muslim driver about Jesus. He was trying to tell me all about the grand scale at the end of time, where your good is weighed against your bad and your eternal destiny hangs in the balance. I wanted him to know about the radical, revolutionary availability of grace. He was telling me neither of us needed it, because if we were religious, we were "good people."

I don't know if my driver's views exactly match up with Islamic orthodoxy. I suspect not. But I do think they basically line up with the orthodoxy of religiosity. It didn't surprise me that a Muslim would think good works is how somebody gets to heaven, because most everybody who thinks there's a heaven thinks good works is the way to get there. But I was astounded the day my daughter told me a teacher at her Christian school, known for its commitment to Reformation theology, told the class that after Christians die, they still have to be punished a little if they've done some *really bad* sins in their life!

That's not only not Reformation theology; it's not Christian theology. That's the kind of junk drawer spirituality that makes sense to everyone's self-righteous moral categories. And it's a shame that it gets smuggled into the Christian subculture, but it's completely understandable. The sheer wonder of undiluted grace creates a moral discombobulation that makes all of us naturally "religious" people uneasy.

To borrow from Matt Popovits's theme, imagine if someone came into your kitchen and stole your junk drawer. It would be a little unnerving, wouldn't it? "I might need those hot sauce packets, zip ties, half-dead batteries, and random keys to locks I can't identify!" The reason the stuff's in the junk drawer is because we don't really need it, but *feel* we might. The same is true of so many of the extraneous religiosities in our lives. They make a kind of emotional sense to us, just as they make an emotional sense to the rest of the world—to people like my Muslim cab driver, for instance. But in the end, holding on to these extrabiblical—and sometimes unbiblical—notions only distracts us from devotion to Jesus.

That's how I felt about that awful purgatory-reminiscent teaching from my daughter's former instructor. To suggest that Christians still need a little punishment after they die for the really bad sins is basically to say that Christ's atoning work on the cross was not sufficient. That his righteousness really isn't perfect. That his blood really isn't that powerful. That all that Jesus did for sinners is somehow *not quite good enough* to satisfy the wrath of God.

The refreshing focus of *Junk Drawer Jesus* is Jesus himself. Page by page, the air gets cleared, the vision gets organized, so that you might be reminded of the goodness, the graciousness, the *enough-ness* of Christ alone.

The author of Hebrews tells us to "lay aside every hindrance and the sin that so easily ensnares us" (12:1). That's what this book aims to do. By getting right to the heart of the good news over and over again, chapter after chapter, Matt pastorally and good-naturedly helps us lay aside the junk threatening to clog up the drawer of our religious lives. It might hurt a little to get rid of it, at least at first. But just like that box of random electric cords dads love to keep in the garage, you don't need all that stuff anyway. There's no real use for it except to get in the way. You're not gonna die if you get rid of it. And in fact, you just might live a little more free.

Jared C. Wilson
Midwestern Seminary
Kansas City, Missouri

The Spiritual Junk Drawer

*"People will do anything, no matter how absurd,
in order to avoid facing their own soul."*

—CARL JUNG

THE JUNK DRAWER. We all have one—or three.

Mine is in the kitchen. It's located to the right of the drawer that holds our dish towels and directly above a large cupboard that houses three things we seldom use: a silver punch bowl, a margarita machine, and an electric griddle. I purchased the griddle on Amazon with the intention that, once it arrived, I would forever wake up early on Saturday mornings to make pancakes for the family. I've used it twice. Maybe it's not a junk drawer for you but the closet in your guest bedroom. It's packed to the brim with clothes you haven't worn in years, items from your old college dorm room, a few unused wedding gifts, and the family printer—which used to sit next to the iMac in the home office before running out of ink sometime before COVID.

The thing about junk drawers and junk closets is that they're not really filled with junk; they're filled with things that we can't quite find a use for day to day but that still hold some kind of meaning for us—or at least we think this stuff could still serve some kind of useful purpose down the road. We don't use the things piled in the drawer and stuffed in the closet, but we can't shake the thought that we *might* need them. We can't bring ourselves to toss it all in the trash.

We just hold on to it.

Spiritual Junk Drawers

I've found the junk drawer to be a fitting metaphor for most people's religious and spiritual world. It seems especially appropriate for those of us who've grown up in the West, where Judeo-Christian foundations and influences have given way to a culture that is increasingly both pluralistic and agnostic.[1] We know of more gods than ever before and believe in them less than we ever have.

A result of this, I contend, is that each of us is the owner of a seemingly random collection of theologies, doctrines, and downright superstitions. It's a "junk drawer" of religious ideas and influences, passed down to us by parents and taught to us by the television shows we stream and the social media influencers we admire. It's a mishmash of quips, phrases, and seemingly wise sayings that have

---

[1] One of the fastest growing religious categories is "spiritual but not religious." An increasing number of Americans, especially younger adults with a Christian upbringing, now say they appreciate a multitude of religious influences but reject adherence to or exclusive alignment with a specific religious group. Caroline Kitchener, 2018. "What It Means To Be Spiritual But Not Religious." The Atlantic. January 11. https://www.theatlantic.com/membership/archive/2018/01/what-it-means-to-be-spiritual-but-not-religious/550337/.

somehow stuck with us. It's the witticisms your grandmother used to toss around with ease that sounded like they came from a religious text. It's an insight gleaned about God from a half-heard sermon at a friend's church you attended for a hot second in the fifth grade. It's mental screenshots of pithy but seemingly profound memes that caught your attention on Instagram and you shared with pride on Facebook. It's the empowering idea you underlined three times in that best-selling book and wrote on a Post-it Note that's now forever affixed to your laptop—something about "living your truth" and "manifesting your dreams."

These are the things stuffed in our spiritual junk drawers, packed in our religious closets. We don't quite know where we got them or even why we keep them. But just like that stash of old clothes or the stew of old phone chargers, empty pens, and half-used batteries sitting in that drawer, something in us says, "This might be useful." And so we hold on.

Wise Examination

If we concede that we all possess a spiritual junk drawer, the next thing to wrestle with is what to do about it. You may be perfectly content just acknowledging its existence and continuing to assume that it's of little consequence to your daily life. But the premise of this book is that spiritual junk drawers should be dealt with, that they must be emptied and their contents examined, and that it's more than worth your time to do a spiritual spring cleaning.

The truth is that the spiritual artifacts you carry do, in fact, influence you. Though they are stuffed in a "drawer," they do not stay there. We are not able to keep these half-truths, assumptions, and old-school superstitions neatly packed in a drawer. When it comes to our psychological lives such compartmentalization is not reality. The junk drawer exists in hearts and minds; hearts and minds that are with us and shape us—albeit subconsciously—at all times. We are never far from the influence of the ideas that we are unwilling to address and refuse to reconsider.

This is especially important since we live in an age when one's spirituality is viewed, even among a majority of Christians, as an entirely private matter.[2] We are far less likely than in previous eras to open up our drawer of spiritual assumptions to the scrutiny and wisdom of others. Instead, we keep the contents of our junk drawer closed, hidden in the dark. Our religious memorabilia, which has a way of seeping into the substance of everyday life, is increasingly protected from the light of engagement with the outside world. So, we better hope that the spiritual stuff we insist on keeping is, in fact, truthful, useful, and good. Otherwise, we've set ourselves up for potential trouble: collecting questionable ideas, allowing them to influence us, and then cutting ourselves off from correction and accountability.

Wisdom tells us that we should be willing to pull open the drawer and examine our spiritual influences and assumptions. It compels us to ask the question, in full view of others, "Is this worth keeping?" I think that if we do, we will find that much of what we hold on to can be tossed to the curb. You might even discover, as many people do when they spring clean, that they quite enjoy the task of doing away

---

[2] "56% of Christians Feel Their Spiritual Life Is Entirely Private," *Barna*, 2022, https://www.barna.com/research/discipleship-friendship/

THE SPIRITUAL JUNK DRAWER

with unnecessary items. There's a freedom in it, a joy to it.[3] You may find that you become something of a spiritual minimalist, interested only in the true essentials, in discerning which of the countless spiritual "truths" available today is most worthy of precious space in your heart and mind.

From my own experience, as you rummage through your spiritual junk drawer, you'll come to the conclusion that this collection hasn't added much in the way of joy and peace to your life. Quite the contrary—it's kept you from discovering the spiritual truths that actually do.

Junk Drawers and Jesus

There may be a lot of Jesus in that junk drawer of yours. A good bit of what you've collected over the years are probably things that you attribute to Christianity or, in some way, associated with the person and work of Jesus Christ. Even these (perhaps especially these) ideas are ones you should extract, examine, and re-assess.

The premise of this book is built on the belief that the truth of Jesus Christ—who he is, what he's accomplished, and what he guarantees about the future—is the ultimate hope for humanity. It contends that what every heart needs to be whole, what every person must encounter to *truly* live, is the message of God's finished work of claiming, saving, and re-creating us through Jesus's life, death,

---

[3] The philosophy of Marie Kondo (konmari.com) comes to mind. There is a need to do to our religious lives what Kondo suggests we do with our possessions, letting go of that which no longer sparks joy, or rings true with what we've come to know of the grace of God. We give thanks for the role certain ideas once played in our lives and then let them go.

resurrection, and return. True spirituality is not adherence to some long list of ethereal principles or foraging for pithy wisdom as we scroll our phones. True spirituality, right religion, is not moral activities we adopt, high-minded attitudes we embrace, or religious platitudes we screenshot and save to our devices.

No, it is a person. It's Jesus.

It is resting in his promises. It is receiving—passively and joyfully—the blessings and benefits of what he's done on behalf of humanity. It is marveling at him, seeing more and more each day our need for him and growing in gratitude for the peace we've found in him. It's my hope that, in the pages that follow, you'll grasp—perhaps for the first time—the simplicity and freedom of a life built on a deep reliance (let's call it faith) upon someone other than yourself, namely Jesus. My hope is that you'll see how different and how much better he is than all of the other spiritual stuff you've chosen to keep and carry.

That being said, just because some of the things in your spiritual junk drawer might bear his name or were handed to you by someone who claimed to be a part of his church doesn't mean they're worth placing in the "keep" pile of our junk drawer deconstruction effort. Much of what is labeled a biblical truth or passed along as Christian teaching, even among people of faith, is the opposite. Under even the tiniest bit of scrutiny, most of it is revealed to be nothing more than basic advice on how to improve our lives or shallow, spiritual-ish notions meant to puff up our egos and make us feel better about ourselves. These quasi-Christian truths are not inherently bad per se, but they're most certainly not of Jesus. In that sense, while not inherently bad, they are—if we don't deal with them—legitimately dangerous as distractions. Everyday advice and shallow sayings are impotent on their own, but wrapped in Christian clothing, they become tempting tenets of faith and objects of trust. And for such usage, they will fail you—and fast. You'll learn the hard way that they cannot deliver you peace for your guilt-ridden conscience, joy for your anxious existence, or life in the face of your death. Not everything in your spiritual junk drawer that claims Christ is of Christ. And if held on to as a source of hope, if we build whatever spiritual assurance we have on our allegiance to such things, they will leave us hurting and hung out to dry in the end. We have to extract and examine all the things in our spiritual collection, especially those that claim a connection to Jesus Christ—because if he is the real thing, then what is most distracting and dangerous is not the obviously outlandish spiritual notion stashed in your supply but the convincing knock-off claiming his name.

The Unreligion

I realize that for some who are reading this book, Christianity—at least Christianity as you've always understood it—is something you've purposely tried to avoid. Maybe your spiritual library is intentionally missing references to Jesus or anything remotely resembling western, American Christian faith. If that's you, thank you for reading.

You're not even through the first chapter, and I've made it clear that this book will attempt to make a case for faith in Jesus Christ over and against every other kind of homespun spirituality common to modern people.

And yet, you're still reading.

You're giving it a shot.

In a time when many would prefer not to have their worldviews and assumptions challenged in any meaningful way lest they cry violence, I consider your continued attention incredibly gracious. So, I mean it: thank you.

I recognize that, when someone has gone to the trouble of curating Jesus *out* of their spiritual storehouse, they have likely done so for a reason. And I recognize that the reasons are not trivial. It's not a decision made lightly. Perhaps it's because the picture of the Christian faith they've received from others feels joyless and oppressive, a long list of expectations and constant moralizing that results in those who follow it feeling awful about themselves or superior to everyone else. It could be that their experience with Christian people is that they seem to lack compassion for others. They see a church that seems to spend a great deal of energy complaining about the ever-broadening cultural acceptance of LGTBQ+ people and the mainstream attention given to their stories and struggles. They take note of the relative silence on the part of many Christians when it comes to issues of race (as well as a hysteria over Critical Race Theory infiltrating our schools), or what seems to be a contradictory obsession with protecting access to guns used to kill kids in schools while ensuring babies make their way safely out of the womb and into the world. They see what is, to them, a litany of frustrating, offensive, and confounding issues attached to Jesus by those who follow him and to which they say, "No, thank you." And so, they remove anything Christian from their collection.

If you're someone who has jettisoned Jesus from your spiritual makeup, my hope is that as we walk through the pages that follow, your generosity toward this topic and this book's thesis will endure.

And that as we move forward, you'll see a fresh and what I believe is a much more accurate picture of Jesus than whatever has been offered to you in the past. But above all, I hope to make clear that Jesus is not only better than the way he's been portrayed to you by others, but he is better than whatever spiritual system or religious worldview you are crafting on your own. The problem with rejecting one religious system in favor of your own is that you still end up with a religious system. You'll think you're assembling something better, but, in fact, you're not. The irony, as we will discover, is that apart from the message of Christ crucified and resurrected for sinners, we end up building the very thing we claim to abhor, a system laden with expectation and burdens, blind spots and bigotries. We build something that robs us of joy and drives us further from the peace and hope we're so desperate to find.

The real Jesus invites us into something altogether different. It turns our spiritual instincts on their head. It completely contradicts the message of the many things we've saved in our spiritual junk drawer. And it is overwhelming in the peace it offers compared to what we craft on our own. The Christian faith rightly experienced is, as Dane Ortlund puts it, the unreligion:

> The ancient Greeks told us to be moderate by knowing our inclinations. The Romans told us to be strong by ordering our lives. Buddhism tells us to be disillusioned by annihilating our consciousness. Hinduism tells us to be absorbed by merging our souls. Islam tells us to be submissive by subjecting our wills. Agnosticism tells us to be at peace by ignoring our doubts. Moralism tells us to be good by discharging our obligations. Only the gospel tells us to be free by acknowledging our failure. Christianity is the unreligion because it is

the one faith whose founder tells us to bring not our doing, but our need.[4]

There is no doing with Jesus. There is just our need. We bring to him our empty hands, our hurting hearts, our grave concerns, and our dying flesh. We offer him our nothing, and he gives us everything we need. Spend some time with that truth. Sit with it for a bit. Dwell on it for a while and tell me it's not better than any other religious notion you've ever encountered.

Bring *nothing*.

Receive *everything*.

Incredible.

A Word of Warning

I hope you are intrigued. I'm praying that you're ready to flip through these pages, rummage through your religious ideas and assumptions, deconstruct your spiritual impulses and your current worldview, and compare it all to the person and work of Jesus Christ.

But before we go further, I have a word of caution—or encouragement; it's really up to you and how you choose to frame it. Here it is: *this won't be easy*.

I will try my best to make it lighthearted and fun, employing silly (and, at times, flimsy) metaphors and analogies for the religious junk we keep and carry. There will be poor attempts at humor and more than a few stories told at my own expense meant to make all of this seem more enjoyable than it would otherwise appear. But the truth

---

[4] Dane Calvin Ortlund, *Defiant Grace: The Surprising Message and Mission of Jesus* (Darlington, England; Carlisle, Pa: Ep Books, 2011).

is that if you take it seriously this will not be an easygoing exercise of sorting items of little regard into various piles on a Saturday afternoon. As mentioned, there is no drawer, just hearts and minds. And a heart is a sacred place to explore. The territory is tender, and all its contents are precious. The instinct of many is not to examine our hearts but to protect them; you could even say avoid them. We have a vague inventory of its contents, but there is also a fear of confronting all that it holds, which is why we so easily embrace distraction via our devices and avoid intense reflection. The legendary psychoanalyst Carl Jung noted our fear of introspection:

> People will do anything, no matter how absurd, in order to avoid facing their own souls. They will practice Indian yoga and all its exercises, observe a strict regimen of diet, learn the literature of the whole world—all because they cannot get on with themselves and have not the slightest faith that anything useful could ever come out of their own souls. Thus the soul has gradually been turned into a Nazareth from which nothing good can come.[5]

Jesus offered something similar when critiquing the religious leaders of his day. Noting that so much of their spirituality was nothing more than window dressing on deep dysfunction, he said:

"You clean the outside of the cup and dish, but inside they are full of greed and self-indulgence. Blind Pharisee! First clean the inside of the cup and dish, so that the outside may become clean as well." (Matthew 23:25-26)

We all begin as blind Pharisees. We will fill our lives with activity in a vain effort to quench our spiritual thirst and avoid addressing

---

[5] Carl Jung, 2014. "Collected Works of C.G. Jung, Volume 12." (Princeton University Press, 2014), p.99.

what lies within. And it gets us nowhere. Worse than that, it drives us further from the peace we need.

The pages that follow are an invitation to open the heart and face the soul. It's a chance to examine "the inside of the cup and dish."

If you take it seriously, it won't be easy. But it will be worth it.

Place your hand on that drawer, clasp the handle that opens the closet, and let's begin.

Taking Inventory

We've established the metaphor of your spiritual junk drawer and laid out the task at hand. It's time to begin sorting through your collection.

We'll start with an idea that's common to everyone. You could call it a foundational tenet in all man-made religion. It's likely hiding somewhere inside your spiritual makeup. And as you'll see, this burdensome but all-too-common idea is what many who attempt to reject religion are actually rebelling against. It's the idea that if someone can just do enough good *for God* then they will be all good *with God*.

The first item in your junk drawer is a scale, meant for adding up all the good that you give to the world.

QUESTIONS TO CONSIDER:

Reflect for a moment on the various influences in your life, from family and friends to popular culture, as well as your upbringing and education. Which has had the greatest impact on your spirituality? Does any specific idea or truth that's important to you come to mind?

Taking a critical look at your spiritual and religious assumptions is a vulnerable task. It requires humility and trust. What are you feeling as we embark on this task? Would you characterize yourself as being cautious and guarded, open and unafraid, or somewhere in between?

The Myth
of the Cosmic Scale

"Have no fear of perfection—you'll never reach it."

—SALVADOR DALI

HAVE YOU EVER MADE pour-over coffee? It's an ordeal.

First, you weigh and grind your beans. You then heat the water to just the right temperature. Next, you add the grinds to a paper filter seated directly on your coffee cup, which has also been heated (you don't want to drink coffee from a cold cup, do you?). You then begin to slowly pour the water over the grinds, making sure to do so at the right speed and allowing the mixture to properly steep between pours. After all that, you wait several minutes for the cup to slowly fill before you finally discard the filter, grab the handle, and take a sip. If you're looking to add time and pretension to your pursuit of a caffeine fix, then look no further.

I was once a pour-over coffee guy. What drew me to it was not just the promise of a great cup of coffee, but the precise process required.

You had to do the right things in the right way. Follow the rules, and the hipster coffee gods might just twirl their ironic mustaches in approval. The task of adding beans to the small, shiny digital scale was particularly enjoyable. There was something very satisfying about dropping bean after bean onto the stainless steel plate until it read exactly "twenty-two grams."

But all that weighing and boiling, pouring and waiting grew tiresome. That shiny little scale is now buried in a drawer beneath wooden spoons and an ice cream scooper. And my morning cup is now made by a one-touch espresso machine. I gave up, burned out on the process required for a great cup of coffee. You could say it became too much of a "grind."

The Cosmic Scale

There's something about a precise process, with a promised reward, that is incredibly alluring. We love the idea of getting things *just right* and of being blessed as a result of our efforts. It invades and affects just about every aspect of our lives. This is why what you'll find in most spiritual junk drawers is some sort of scale.

This scale represents a belief, held by many, that Someone out there is scrupulously weighing our actions, both good and bad. The goal of life then, the substance of our religious expression, consists of making sure that we carefully load more good works than bad ones, more nice things than nasty things, onto this cosmic scale. And if we do manage to tip things into our favor, proving that we've mostly been good, then God (the Universe, our conscience, the culture, or whoever we believe is minding the scale) will reward us. And the rewards vary, depending on who you believe is tending the scale. Count out enough good with your life, and you could walk away with anything from a solid night's sleep brought to you by a clear conscience, to the applause of your peers given for surpassing the expectations of cultural kindness, to heaven itself and an eternity of joy doled out by a deity who demands we do good.

Whatever the reward and whoever is measuring, the resultant dynamic is the same. Life becomes a spirituality of the scale. We are constantly cognizant of what we are "putting into the world" and wondering whether we are good enough. We cannot shake the notion that all of life is being weighed and measured and that we must do our best to tip things in our favor.

Our daily lives are shaped by this notion of a cosmic scale in ways that we easily overlook. Think, for example, about the way you navigate food surrounding the holidays. If you're like me, you become hyper-conscious about all that you're tempted to eat as you hop from celebration to celebration. And you feel pressure, after indulging at the office holiday party, to hold back when opening presents with the in-laws two nights later. At one party, you convince yourself, "It's Christmas! I'll be *bad* and hit the buffet twice." But at the next, you say, "I've gotta be *good*. I'll limit myself to just one of grandma's famous ham rolls and a single glass of wine." Sure, it's a trivial example, but you see the dynamic, don't you?

Or, think about the last time you treated a coworker poorly. On the long drive home from the office, reflecting on the day, you felt a pang of guilt for being overly terse with Terry in accounting. And so you decide, as you pull into the driveway, that you're going to be extra kind to your spouse and kids. Why? Because you love them? Well, sure. But that's not the primary motivation. Tonight, you're going to be Super

Dad because you're trying to convince yourself, after being a jerk to Terry, that you're a good person. So, you load up the dishwasher after dinner without being asked, and you take the lead in preparing the kids for bed—showers, story time, and all. Doing so makes you feel better. It numbs your guilt. And it tips the scale.

Or, perhaps you carry some guilt from a series of choices you made earlier in life. You did things that you not only regret but that you feel immense shame over. But, looking at you now, no one would know that your heart is heavy, and your past is shocking. That's because you've spent the last few decades taking every opportunity to do the right thing and follow the rules—not just because it's the right thing to do, but because you're trying to bury your past sins under your present obedience, hoping no one will see what you've done or who you used to be. You're balancing the scale.

In big and small things—even in the most mundane of things—we are drawn toward a tendency to measure good against bad. Rather than address the real issue, by apologizing to the coworker or confessing our long-held guilt to someone who can absolve us, we try to "fix" things by spooning just a little more goodness, obedience, kindness—anything—onto the scales of life.

Not Good Enough

The Christian faith tells us that this approach to life—however common—is, to put it mildly, problematic. The problem is not in believing that there's someone watching all that we do or that there will be, in the end, some kind of accounting of our good and bad choices. Indeed, God *is* watching what we do. And he tells us, quite clearly, that "judgment day" is a real thing.[1] No, the problem is in our belief that we can do enough good to balance out our lives at all. The Christian faith makes it clear that we simply cannot be good enough.

The historic Christian faith, rooted in the words of scripture and focused on the person and work of Jesus, paints an awful (albeit accurate) picture of humanity. We are more than just a little messed up. We are more than merely imperfect. There is a critical corruption within us that runs so deep, and which produces motives, thoughts, and actions so offensive in comparison to the holiness of God[2] that no amount of "acts of kindness" can counterbalance it. You can't buy enough Tom's shoes or like enough inspirational content on social media to make a dent. And while we might initially bristle at such a negative take, if we sit with it long enough and reflect honestly on the choices we've made and the inner workings of our own hearts, we can't help but agree that it's true. Negative, but true.

Think of it like this. Not long ago, I was grocery shopping. But this was not your quick trip to grab a few items; the cart was overflowing. It was the kind of shopping trip where it takes you a full ten minutes just to load up the conveyor belt for checkout, plus a short break to catch your breath. When it came time to pay, I pulled out my bank

---

[1] In the second article of the Apostles' Creed Christians confess that, "[Jesus] ascended into heaven and sits at the right hand of God, the Father Almighty. From there He will come to judge the living and the dead." Likewise, Jesus himself offers this: "Therefore you also must be ready, for the Son of Man is coming at an hour you do not expect." (Matthew 24:44)

[2] The evils of humanity are described like this in the story of Noah and the flood in the Old Testament: "The Lord saw that the wickedness of man was great in the earth, and that every intention of the thoughts of his heart was only evil continually." (Genesis 6:5) It's harsh, yes. But let's be brutally honest; it's also accurate.

card, inserted the chip, punched in my code, and then heard a beep. But it wasn't the good beep; it was a different beep, a bad beep. The screen on the card reader said, "Declined." I tried the card again and received the same bad beep—"Declined." I could sense the people in line behind me reacting to what was happening. One customer was annoyed, and another seemed sympathetic. I was supremely embarrassed. I knew that I had more than enough money; it had to be a mistake. Sure enough, the bank had flagged another transaction as fraudulent and shut down my card without telling me. But none of that mattered in the moment. It was the only card I had with me. Instantly, it hit me: "I can't pay." And the thing about grocery stores these days is that they *insist* on being paid for the food you're trying to take home. No amount of explanation or pleading with the kid behind the register would do me any good. I either had to find a way to pay for my mountain of groceries or go home empty-handed. I went home with nothing.

We go through life piling our "cart" high with all kinds of stuff: our words and actions, thoughts and decisions, successes and regrets. And we pull up to the checkout, expecting that we'll be able to pull a long list of good deeds out of our purse or pocket and somehow make payment for all that we've loaded into our cart. But if we try to give God our goodness, we'll get declined. We may have a load of good intentions and great excuses to hand him too, but none of it will matter—there's far too much stuff piled up on the conveyor belt. We don't have enough good actions, good words, good intentions, or good excuses to cover it all. We've piled up more than we can afford. We simply can't pay.

It's tempting to think God is a jerk for being unwilling to accept whatever measly offerings we can muster. After all, isn't he loving? Isn't forgiveness kind of his thing? Why is he keeping a ledger in the first place and exacting any kind of "payment" at all? Such questions are understandable, but they fail to take into account a few important things, like the holiness of God, the deep depravity of humankind, and the concept of justice, to name a few. If God exists, then he is, by definition, perfect, pure, and good beyond our ability to grasp.[3] He's not being finicky with his unwillingness to accept our good works as payment; he's just being holy. Likewise, we are not merely good people who make a few mistakes every now and then—it's much worse than that. There is a deep dysfunction within us,[4] giving rise to truly terrible choices. It infects even our most noble deeds with self-serving intent and infuses all that we think and do with an iniquitous flavor. And then there's justice—a concept that receives near universal veneration and that we label as essential to a moral universe. And indeed, it is. But does justice actually exist if the God at the center

---

[3] "Who is like you, O Lord, among the gods? Who is like you, majestic in holiness, awesome in glorious deeds, doing wonders?" (Exodus 15:11) Surrounded by so much that's broken and dysfunctional, the holiness and perfection of God are difficult, if not impossible, concepts for us to fully appreciate. And yet, we intuitively seem to understand that if God does exist, and if he is to be worthy of our praise, then he must be nothing other than, nothing less than perfect.

[4] "... as it is written: 'None is righteous, no, not one; no one understands; no one seeks for God. All have turned aside; together they have become worthless; no one does good, not even one.'" (Romans 3:10-12) It has been said that the bad news of Christianity is worse than you want to think but the good news of the Christian faith is better than you can possibly fathom. We are not merely a people who make mistakes; we are utterly corrupt. All of us. It's that bad. But the love of God in Jesus Christ is such that despite this complete corruption we are forgiven, accepted, and made his own.

of the Universe—to whom all things are accountable, by whom all things are measured, and against whom we've all sinned—ignores our evils and offends his own holiness by accepting anything less than full payment for all that's gone wrong? If there's no justice for God, then there's no reason to insist on it for ourselves.

The bottom line is this: God is holier than we can imagine, and humankind is more awful than we can begin to grasp or admit. As a result, it's truly ludicrous to think that we can somehow make it right, tip the scale, or pay for it all by just trying to be better people. Being good enough will simply never be good enough.

On the question of what is truly "good enough," Martin Luther, the great reformer, offers some helpful distinctions. In a 1518 sermon entitled "Two Kinds of Righteousness," Luther distinguishes between what he calls alien righteousness and proper righteousness. Proper righteousness are the good things we do in our everyday lives. It's our active goodness, you might say. It's the help you afford a coworker, the kindness extended to a stranger, and your refusal to cheat on your taxes. Alien righteousness, however, is neither active nor earned, but rather is bestowed and infused from the outside, and therefore "alien." It is a passive state of being right with God. It is not a medal you win but an unmerited status that you receive.

In the Christian faith no amount of proper righteousness can amount to a right relationship with God. You may indeed be a fantastic human being, with an impeccable resume of good deeds. But it will not make you holy, whole, and faultless in the eyes of an almighty God. These two kinds of righteousness aren't even on the same scale; they are of two different natures. One is a wage that you earn by being a nice guy, and the other is a gift that you're given through faith in Christ's goodness, alone.

The Solution

The cosmic scale is built on the notion that your relationship with God is up to you. The power is in your hands. But, as we can now see, that's not true; the power is and always has been in God's hands. He's the one who's been wronged; he's the one who "reads the scale," and therefore, he's the one with all the power. And the only question—the truly important question—is what is he going to do with it? Will he hold each of us accountable for our failures, or will he forsake the whole system and get us off the hook? Will he demand justice, or will he offer us mercy?

This very question rises to the surface almost immediately in the Christian scriptures. Within the first few chapters of the biblical narrative, Adam and Eve have blown it, grieving the God who placed them in the Garden of Eden by doing the *one* thing they were told not to do. In a garden of "yes," they insisted on eating from the one tree marked, "no." And on and on the rebellion continues. This first family eventually grows into the nation known as Israel, and though they are God's own people, they are still (along with the rest of humanity) Adam and Eve's descendants. It's thousands of years of dysfunction played out on the pages of the Old Testament. Over and over, God makes a promise to his people, he protects and provides for them, rescues and cares for them, and they respond with faithlessness and idolatry. And while Israel faced many repercussions for their dysfunction, they remained God's people, complete with relentlessly refreshed promises and continually renewed covenants. And yet, hanging over it all is the same question we've been wrestling with: "But what will

God do in the *end*?" And there will be an end. And on that day, what will the last word be: justice or mercy?

It reminds me of when I was a young boy, and my brothers and I would get into trouble with my mom. She was a stay-at-home parent who spent almost every waking hour of her life making sure that her boys didn't destroy each other or our small house. It was a particularly tough task in the summer months when we'd all be stuck inside the same four walls while Dad was off at work. Fights erupted, tears were shed, elbows were thrown, and one time, a golf club went through a bedroom door. We were—how should I put this?—awful.

When at her absolute wit's end, Mom would resort to threats. Her favorite and most effective went something like this, "If you boys don't cut it out, I'm going to call your father." To no one's surprise, we did not cut it out, and my father's work was regularly interrupted with the latest story of how his three sons were making summer a nightmare for the love of his life. Once the inevitable call was placed, we would wait and wonder: "What's Dad going to do when he gets home?" The question was fair because it was never a given as to how my dad would respond. Sometimes, "Justice Dad" would show up, shouting his displeasure and grounding us from every conceivable summer joy. To be honest, Justice Dad was what we deserved. But other times, it was "Mercy Dad." He would arrive home angry, looking much like Justice Dad, but upon gathering us boys together to announce our punishment, he would lean in close and say, "Look, it's been a long day; I don't have it in me to be angry tonight." And then, placing a very firm hand on our shoulders, he'd say, "I just want your mom to be happy. So, stop being jerks, work up some tears, and go give her a hug. And if she asks, tell her I was furious." Mercy Dad was awesome.

Which God will humankind get in the end? Will we get the God of justice who gives us what we and all those who've come before us deserve? Or will we receive mercy? The world waited for millennia for an answer to that question. And then one day, it arrived. That's right—we already have an answer to this all-important question. The Christian faith teaches us that the answer is not justice or mercy. It's both. It's Christ.

In the person and work of Jesus Christ, God himself has come forward and cut the tension created by the cosmic scale. With his perfectly obedient life, Jesus tipped the scale completely toward the good. And with his sacrificial death, he took the punishment for our having piled it high with nothing but bad. Not only that, but in his resurrection, he showed that the curse of death—a plague upon humankind for our continuous rebellion—had been broken. And all that he's done—the living, the dying, the rising—gets credited to us, gifted to us, by grace through faith[5] alone. That's it. There's no begging or bartering or promising to "do better." There's just faith. Dependent upon Christ, all that he's accomplished becomes ours.

And knowing this, we can relax. We can relax because it means the cosmic scale has been put out of commission, and the big question of "what will I get from God in the end?" has been answered. The

---

[5] "For I am not ashamed of the gospel, for it is the power of God for salvation to everyone who believes, to the Jew first and also to the Greek. For in it the righteousness of God is revealed from faith for faith, as it is written, 'The righteous shall live by faith.'" (Romans 1:16-17) These words of Paul were critical to what would become known as the Protestant Reformation of the sixteenth century. Martin Luther, upon studying these words and others, would rediscover the good news that mankind is made right with God not by any good work or good intention but simply by faith in the promise of Jesus Christ.

ending, that moment of judgment, has come and gone in the life, death, and resurrection of Jesus Christ. Justice has been done, and mercy has been won for you, for all, in him.[6]

Fear of God

Once you realize that the scale can be pulled from your spiritual junk drawer and tossed in the trash, everything changes. The first and most substantial shift is in how we approach God. Whereas we once saw God as someone to appease with our meticulous performance or to ignore in bitter rebellion, the lights are now on, and we now see a much better, more satisfying way of dealing with the Divine. We no longer need to satisfy him or assert our will against him. Instead, we are free to *fear* him.

Let me explain.

Psalm 103 is a marvelous prayer. It paints a powerful picture of God's attitude toward his people and how he deals with us despite our incessant struggle with sin. It also illustrates what our faith-filled response to his divine compassion and forbearance should look like. In the context of our conversation, one line in particular stands out:

> As a father shows compassion to his children, so the Lord shows compassion to those who fear him. (Psalm 103:13)

What does God deserve from us? Our fear. What are we, as the recipients of all that's been accomplished in Christ, free to give him? Our

---

[6] "[God] does not deal with us according to our sins, nor repay us according to our iniquities." (Psalm 103:10) Christ is the fulfillment of this promise made in the Psalms, the prayer book of the Old Testament. Christ has been dealt with according to our sins and repaid according to our iniquities, or awful behavior. He received what we deserve, and now we get to enjoy the forgiveness and the freedom that he has earned.

fear. But this is not fear of punishment; this is no terror of potential pain. Remember, we get to understand these words, and all of scripture, in light of Christ. And in Christ, any payment or punishment for sin has already been offered and accepted. God is out of that business. So, this must be some other kind of fear.

Consider the entire verse: "*As a father ... to his children ...*" God is a perfect parent, and we are his cherished children. What this must be is a fear soaked in the knowledge of his unending love, overflowing with gratitude for all he provides and infused with the kind of peace that comes from knowing all of his power is used *for us* and not against us. It's less "fear" in the modern sense and more awe—awe of the lengths he will go to love us and of the restraint he shows in not rejecting or abandoning us. It's being made breathless by the fact that God could, in his glory and with his power, rightly judge and destroy us. But he doesn't. Instead, he uses all that he is and all that he has to *bless* us. That's humbling. That's fear. That's what he deserves.

Practically speaking, this kind of fear lived out on a daily basis is what Christians call worship. Worship is more than going to church on Sunday, although that's certainly a part of it. Worship is an attitude, a posture we take in heart and mind in all that we do. It's an understanding that everything, every breath we take and every task we tackle with respect to God is not a chore meant to appease him, a token to persuade him, or even an act of defiance to unseat him. No. All that we do is a "thank you" to him. We are humbled by how he loves us, and, as a result, our entire lives become praise.

Discipleship then—the process of being formed as a follower of Jesus—is in part about adopting this heart of fear, this continual posture of praise. The notion of God as a taskmaster is a hard one to kick. We return to it easily. And so, we must[7] regularly reframe our intentions, especially in the aftermath of sin and struggle, around the truth that justice and mercy have already been accomplished in Christ. It means asking ourselves some deep questions about what we are doing or thinking and how it relates to God: am I, freshly aware of my sin, now seeking to appease him; am I digging my heels and asserting my agency in defiance of him, or is what I'm doing now a "thank you" to him, knowing that, *despite my incredible dysfunction,* I still belong to and am beloved by him?

I encourage you, as you go through this week, to test this out. As you drive home from work with a heart full of regret over how the day has gone, or as you catch yourself reflecting on some sins of the past while emptying the dishwasher, ask yourself: "Why am I about to do whatever it is that I do next? Am I balancing the scale? Am I rebelling against it? Or am I rejoicing, knowing that no matter my issues, God shows compassion to his children?" I pray it's the latter. And if it's not, no worries—just confess it. Pause in prayer and, with your heart holding on to Christ, admit it. And then be confident that even your unwillingness to worship is forgiven on account of Christ. And may *that* fill you with awe and move you to praise.

---

[7] The Christian scriptures teach that even our repentance, our returning to God, is a gift. It's a work of God in us and not something we've conjured up on our own. Indeed, one's entire journey of sanctification (of being transformed by God) is done by the power of the Holy Spirit, who is promised to be at work in all those who have faith in Christ and have been baptized into his name.

(Real) Love for Others

When religion is about balancing the scales, it not only distorts our relationship with God, but it changes how we deal with others. It influences every interaction, be it with family, friends, coworkers, or total strangers. A life lived to tip the divine scales is a life lived with a self-serving agenda. Every good thing we do for others, all the love we show and kindness we pour out, is not done for the flourishing of that other person. Deep down, because of the scale, it's actually done *for us*. We *need* to love others. We *must* love others. Why? So that God will love and accept us. The neighbor we help becomes a means to our own end. We're not loving them; we're using them.

Likewise, because the myth of the Cosmic Scale is built on a transactional view of our relationship with God, we should not be surprised if the notion of transactional love works its way into our other relationships. If it's good enough for God only to reward those who meet his standards, then what's to stop us from engaging in the same dynamic with our spouse or children? I mean, if *God* is doing it, then shouldn't we? And yet, most everyone alive and interacting with other, profoundly disturbed human beings for more than five minutes knows that there's something untenable—and dare I say, evil—about such a graceless, self-serving, "What's in it for me?" approach to relationships. There's at least one surefire way to destroy a marriage, a friendship, a relationship with your child: fairness. Insist on making all things equal and that the blessings and burdens involved balance out for all parties. To say or imply to another person, "As long as you're good to me, I'll be good to you," is to give that relationship a lethal injection. It leaves no room whatsoever for mercy. If you're going to be in a relationship of any kind with another sinner, it requires that you find a way to love them despite their inability to balance the scales. It can't be transactional; it has to be sacrificial.

Of course, that's what God the Father has done for the world in sending his Son, Jesus Christ. Look again at Psalm 103:

> ...the Lord shows compassion to those who fear him. For he knows our frame; he remembers that we are dust. (Psalm 103:13-14)

God has refused to play fair with us, to be transactional with us. He "knows our frame," recognizing that we are dust, fragile and incapable of giving him fully what it is he deserves. To insist that we did would have spelled the end for humanity and ensured the end of his relationship with us. So, instead of extracting payment from you and me, he took it from his own son who could afford it.

Knowing and believing this has the power to transform all of our earthly relationships. We are off the hook for having to balance the scale with God; we have received a mountain of mercy that we don't deserve and are guaranteed a bright future with a Heavenly Father who works all things for our good.[8] We are now free to offer some semblance of the same to those around us. Christ has won all that we need and gifted it to us through faith. What else could we possibly

---

[8] "And we know that for those who love God all things work together for good, for those who are called according to his purpose." (Romans 8:28) To be clear, this verse is not saying that everything that happens in life will *be* good. Many terrible and tragic things happen. But rather that God is so powerful and so loving that he uses even the terrible and the tragic *for* good, according to his mysterious will. This is part of how Jesus reigns victoriously over our broken world, prior to his return. Having defeated sin and death through weakness and seeming defeat on the cross, he is still at work in hardship and pain, using it all to bring about his ultimate plans and purpose.

need to extract from friends and family that would make harming the relationship worth it? What worthwhile reason could we have for desperately trying to ensure that all is fair, and the scales are balanced between us and our coworkers? I mean, *really*? We are set free, through Christ, to abandon the scale in our earthly relationships and simply love our neighbor for our neighbor's sake.

Truly Enough

There's something about a precise process with a promised reward that is incredibly alluring. We love the idea of getting things *just right* and of being blessed as a result of our efforts. It can be lived out with great satisfaction in hobbies, projects, personal goals, and professional development. Being meticulous and exacting can lead to wonderful things when brewing coffee, building furniture, training for a marathon, and hitting your sales goals. But it's death to relationships. Minding a scale will get you nowhere with God, and it will ruin things with others.

In the movie musical *The Greatest Showman*, famed nineteenth-century soprano Jenny Lind (played by Rebecca Ferguson and voiced by Loren Allred) performs the song "Never Enough." The song is beautifully delivered, stunning the crowd and stealing the heart of P.T. Barnum, played by Hugh Jackman. While the performance is mesmerizing, the message of the song is heartbreaking. The lyrics reveal a young woman inviting a lover to remain by her side, believing that, without this relationship, her deep need for acclaim is doomed to go unsatisfied:

All the shine of a thousand spotlights
All the stars we steal from the night sky
Will never be enough

Never be enough
Towers of gold are still too little
These hands could hold the world but it'll
Never be enough

But the pressure placed on the lover she's serenading is too immense. "Stay with me, or I will never know joy. I could hold the world, but without you, it won't be enough." The future of her relationship is foreshadowed by her request. If Lind is not affirmed by "a thousand spotlights," then what hope does her boyfriend have of making her happy? The starlet's appetite for approval is simply too insatiable.

There is something familiar to each of us in Jenny Lind's song. The desire to perform and earn praise, all while fearing that who we are, what we offer, and what we win as a result may "never be enough," is something that most, when honest, can relate to. And yet the character's instinct to seek satisfaction in a person rather than in the praise her performance can garner is actually headed in the right direction. Accomplishments will never satisfy; only a certain person will. But it's not a romantic interest, and it's certainly not an already married circus producer. What truly satisfies is faith in the person of Jesus Christ. His performance pleases the only Audience that matters and earns you the approval that truly counts. Apart from faith in Christ, whatever you do will simply never be enough.

Thankfully, all such performing—the life on the scale—has been rendered obsolete. And the questions that come with it, about justice and mercy, have all been answered in our favor. Earning and proving in regard to God are over. Sure, you can keep some scales around if you're trying to track your weight or brew the perfect cup of coffee, but it's not needed for your spirituality. We just don't measure anymore; instead, we worship, we love, and we trust that, because of Christ, we *are* good.

Taking Inventory

The burdensome lie that we must somehow please the gods with our good deeds is an essential one to dismantle. But as we turn to other items in the drawer, be aware that this idea of "salvation by works" is a tricky one, easily creeping back into our religious frameworks, even if we don't consider ourselves all that religious.

Take, for example, what one could call secular spirituality. Secular spirituality is made up of a number of things, such as the values-of-the-moment championed in mass media, the various moral imperatives campaigned on by politicians, and the causes that move celebrities to post tear-filled pleas online. While sometimes espousing noble values and often imploring us to take up just causes, it is fueled by fear and guilt. Secular spirituality relentlessly sends the message that we must do our part to appease (the god of) progress and prove ourselves to be good, lest we be damned to the hell of being labeled ignorant, uncaring, or part of the problem. It's a potent force, but don't be fooled. It's the same toxicity we addressed earlier, albeit in a different, less traditionally religious wrapper.

We now shift our focus to a close cousin of what we just discussed. Whereas the scale dealt with the idea of offering good works to God, the next item we'll examine looks at the notion that we must constantly measure and assess our spiritual progress. It's an impulse that if left unaddressed can rob your life of much peace and joy. It's time for us to deconstruct our rulers.

QUESTIONS TO CONSIDER:

Is there something in your life about which you are a perfectionist, some task for which "good enough" is never good enough? If so, why do you think you're so hard on yourself, and perhaps others, about that particular thing?

How does the notion of "throwing out the scale" in regard to God make you feel? Does it strike you as liberating, or as cheap grace and too good to be true?

Is it your instinct to see God as demanding perfection or as eager to forgive?

THREE

Of Mountains
and Measurement

"Am I a good person? Deep down, do I even really want to be a good person, or do I only want to seem like a good person so that people (including myself) will approve of me? Is there a difference?"

—DAVID FOSTER WALLACE

IN JUNE OF 2017, something truly incredible happened: Alex Honnold, an American rock climber, completed a free solo climb of El Capitan in Yosemite National Park. A free solo climb utilizes no ropes, no anchors, and no safety gear of any kind. Honnold climbed the 3,000-foot granite monolith using just his hands and feet. It had never been done before. For comparison, a 2015 free climb (with protective gear and safety rope) of El Capitan's Dawn Wall by another mountaineer was widely celebrated for having been completed in eight days. Alex Honnold completed his climb in just three hours and fifty-six minutes. It was astounding and *crazy* (no ropes!?).[1]

---

[1] *Free Solo*, by National Geographic Documentary Films, is incredible. It cannot be recommended enough. Although, fair warning, your heart will race as you watch Honnold's journey to the top of El Capitan.

We are prone to understand the Christian faith a bit like climbing El Capitan. Sure, we are forgiven members of God's family through faith in Jesus Christ, but that's just the beginning. It's base camp, if you will. Our job is to climb higher, like Honnold, with our own hands and feet. We must get even closer to God through moral excellence, biblical knowledge, a profound prayer life, deeply emotional experiences in worship, or social activism. And at the summit is a fuller, richer experience of God and his gifts. At the top, prayers rarely go unanswered, personal success is secured, and God's presence is not only palpable but pervasive.

The Ruler

Buried somewhere in your spiritual junk drawer is a ruler—the wooden kind used in grade school way back in the day. The nice ones had painted, durable hash markings for accurate measurements along with a metal edge along the side, which was useful for drawing perfectly straight lines for the panels in your homemade comic book *and* for turning the ruler into a surprisingly effective sword—great for defending yourself against a tormenting older sibling. Pulling it out, you see that it's covered in all kinds of scribbles, scratches, and dents—signs that it's been used for many a measurement, a lot of sketches, and a good deal of swordplay. In chapter two, we discussed the myth of the Cosmic Scale, the notion that God is weighing our good works, measuring our performance, and rewarding accordingly. And while it is similar, the ruler represents *our* desire to measure. Specifically, it represents a lure we feel to measure our religious progress and the lie we buy that says, "You must climb higher. You must see how far you've scaled and then keep on climbing. The summit, with all its glory, awaits."

Endless Assessment

In certain Christian traditions, the importance given to the ruler, to endlessly assessing your own progress, is rather pronounced. For example, in many Pentecostal circles, there is an intense emphasis on the Holy Spirit, the third person of the Trinity. In this tradition, being promised the gift of the Holy Spirit by virtue of one's baptism in water and God's Word is not enough. One must also be "baptized in the Spirit," which is thought to be distinct from water baptism and involves the display of certain "charismata" or powerful gifts such as prophecy, healing, and speaking in tongues. The manifestation of these gifts serves as proof of God's presence in the believer's life and helps attract others toward the church.

An often-used analogy in Pentecostal circles is that of a glass of water. The believer is the glass, and the Spirit is the water. Everyone, by virtue of their faith, has a little. Some have more than others, but the goal is to be filled to the rim, so filled that at any time, water—the Spirit—might spill out of you, signaling God's presence, power, and approval. The implication is that it's not enough to merely have the Spirit. For the Pentecostal, the important question every believer must continually ask is, "Am I full of the Spirit?" In other words, take out the ruler and measure; then, no matter what you find, keep growing and going and getting more.

The call to endless spiritual self-assessment is also prominent among those who preach what's referred to as the prosperity gospel, also known as the gospel of health and wealth or the Word of Faith movement.[2] For those who ascribe to the prosperity gospel, salvation is just the beginning. God has wealth, success, and all kinds of worldly joys waiting for you. All you need to do is claim them, which typically involves using the power of your faith to manifest them—by speaking, praying, and tithing—into existence. And if you're not seeing the fruit of God's blessings in your life, the problem, according to this school of theology, most likely is *you*. You need to believe more genuinely, pray more fervently, or give more generously.

But, as stated earlier, the obsession with the ruler is something we all struggle with, regardless of which theological tribe we belong to. Not a day goes by where each one of us isn't tempted to pull it out of the drawer. For example, think back to the last difficulty you endured. Perhaps the person you were dating suddenly ignored your texts and began to leave you "on read." Or your job, which you just so happened to enjoy, got cut as part of a "reduction in labor costs." Or your health, which had been improving, suffered a major setback. If you're the typical person of faith, part of your response to such difficulty is to begin asking some spiritual questions, but not just any questions. Struggling to make sense of our problems, we assume a lack of growth, effort, or character is the culprit. In other words, we pull out the ruler:

Did I not pray enough?

Am I not a good person—is this some kind of punishment?

If I had served more or given more, would this have happened?

---

[2] For a history of the prosperity gospel and its ties to the Pentecostal tradition see Kate Bowler's *Blessed: A History of the American Prosperity Gospel*, from Oxford University Press.

In the presence of pain, most everyone takes out the ruler and assesses themselves, wondering whether a little more progress or a few more inches "up the mountain" would have spared them from pain.

Put It Away

It's safe to say that the scriptures give a very clear answer to all of this. In multiple places, God goes out of his way, in one form or another, to say that he despises the use of the ruler and that he cannot stand "mountain climbers"—metaphorically speaking, of course. Although, as a personal aside, have you ever *met* a mountain climber? They're like runners—they're *always* telling you about it:

You: *"Hey Greg! It's been a while. How are the kids?"*

Greg: *"Funny you ask. So, the other day, I was nearing the summit of—"*

You: *"This is why it's been a while."*

I digress. God makes it clear that the whole notion of measuring your progress and climbing to attain more of what he promises is just plain ludicrous. Actually, you could argue that it makes him downright angry.

In his letter to the Galatians, Paul is writing to a young church that had become deeply confused. Their spiritual health and, quite frankly, their salvation were being threatened by the presence of false teachers shilling a dangerous distortion of the Christian Gospel. These teachers, it seems, were attempting to convince the church that having faith in Jesus simply wasn't enough. Such an understanding was too basic, they said. It lacked wisdom and maturity. They needed to do more. Specifically, the Christians were urged to adopt certain practices from the Jewish faith, such as circumcision, to be legitimately considered followers of Jesus. Paul wasn't having it.

Have you ever heard or witnessed something so egregious, so offensive or destructive, that it interrupted your plans? The danger or stupidity of it was so profound that your errands would have to wait, or the kids would have to be late to practice because the basic rules of human decency demanded that you speak up, step up, or otherwise intervene? That was Paul. The moment he heard about what was going on in Galatia, he thought, "Well, dang. Change of plans. I've gotta shut that down right now."

Paul had planted the Galatian church by preaching the gospel of salvation by grace through faith in Jesus Christ *alone*. After learning what was being taught and believed post his departure, he acted quickly, writing a letter in which he called out the lies and defended his teaching. The tone of the letter is urgent and passionate. This was clearly no small problem to Paul. With the formal greeting barely concluded, Paul unloads. He shares his shock and dismay that the church has bought into a message so contrary to the one he first preached to them:

> I am astonished that you are so quickly deserting him who called you in the grace of Christ and are turning to a different gospel ... even if we or an angel from heaven should preach to you a gospel contrary to the one we preached to you, let him be accursed. (Galatians 1:6, 8)

Two chapters later, and Paul is still at it. He now shifts his efforts to reminding the church of Christ's once and for all sacrifice, of how they themselves had entered God's grace (by hearing the Gospel), and of the curse that comes with connecting one's reception of grace to rules, laws, and traditions:

> O foolish Galatians! Who has bewitched you? It was before your eyes that Jesus Christ was publicly portrayed as crucified. Let me ask you only this: Did you receive the Spirit by works of the law or by hearing with faith?...For all who rely on works of the law are under a curse; for it is written, "Cursed be everyone who does not abide by all things written in the Book of the Law, and do them." Now it is evident that no one is justified before God by the law, for "The righteous shall live by faith." (Galatians 3:1-2; 10-11)

"Let's think this through," Paul says. "You didn't enter God's family through your effort, by keeping the law. It was through faith in the promise (that I preached to you!) of the crucified and resurrected Jesus. That's it! So, what makes you think that the game has changed? Do you really believe you're going to get more from God by piling traditions and expectations on top of the work of Jesus?"

Paul even goes as far as to add that, if they were to buy into the false gospel being peddled in Galatia, they were inviting a curse upon their lives. If one's assurance of salvation is centered on adherence to certain rites, rules, and regulations, then one would live under an impossible burden and die in defeat. The pressure to perform would cast a shadow over their life, with failure finally confronting them in death. They would stand before God, with their efforts in hand, only to learn in judgment that it had just not been enough. And that, for Paul, was a curse.

Paul is pleading with the Galatians (and with us) to understand that bloodying your hands through climbing and striving, relentlessly measuring your progress, and pondering your assent will get you nowhere. You will never arrive. You won't even come close. We simply don't get closer to God, in any way, by doing more for God. The Christian message rejects any and all earning, climbing, and laying claim to God or his gifts through our efforts. Instead, we are taught that we bring *nothing* to God yet receive *everything* from *God* through faith alone in the Son of God, Jesus Christ. That's it. So, put that ruler away.

Reasonable Questions

At this point, you might find yourself asking a few questions.

You might be wondering about the importance of spiritual growth—after all, shouldn't we be striving to become more like Jesus? And what about all the things that the scriptures encourage us to do, like confess our sins, be constant in prayer, and love our neighbor? Does caring about these things mean that we've pulled out the ruler? Does taking the call to Christian living seriously equal obsessing about our progress up some spiritual mountain and expecting something special from God?

Or, you might be wondering about the connection, if any, that exists between the difficult things we experience and our performance in the faith. I mean, it is very easy to connect the two. Are we *sure* our growth and obedience don't affect the number of burdens we avoid and blessings we attain? These are all reasonable questions. Let's start with the latter: making sense of the problems we face.

Problems and Pain

The primary reason bad things happen is that the world we live in and the reality we experience have been utterly overwhelmed by the effects of sin. It's as simple as that. Every atom of creation and every aspect of life was knocked off-kilter the moment sin entered the world. Nothing is or operates as it should, not us as people and not anything else. *That's* why bad things happen. It's not that God is withholding his blessings from you or is mad and punishing you. God is not standing back and waiting for you to prove that you're above the dysfunctional fray so that he can unlock an easier life for you the same way you'd level up in a video game. And it's certainly not the case that he's making things more difficult for you because you've failed to follow the rules. Bad things happen because this is a world, and we are a people still reeling with the effects of sin. That's it.

Spiritual Growth

When it comes to the question of our spiritual growth, it's helpful to remember that God is our father, and we are his children. This is not a throw-away metaphor. God employs it so that we might derive substantial peace and understanding about who he is and how life works.

How do good fathers treat their children? Specifically, how do they inspire growth and good behavior in their children? Sure, some dads might offer an incentive. I'm guilty of bribing my son to act sane at a Walmart with the promise of waffle fries. "Be good for just a minute, and I promise we'll hit up Chick-fil-A on the ride home." But here's what a good dad *never* says: "Sure, you're my son. But don't assume you have my affection, my provision, and my protection. That's extra. You've got to earn it." What kind of father would withhold the foundational elements of love and care based on performance? Not only that, but what kind of dad would use it as a means of manufacturing growth and obedience? That's horrific. That's abusive.

God, being a good father, *withholds* nothing and *demands* nothing in order to love, care, and provide for his children. And it's the experience of this truth—the preemptive, unearned, and constant fatherly love of God—that stirs up actual, authentic growth in us. We do not grow *for* love but *from* it. Knowing what we possess inspires who we should become. We want to grow, and we aim to obey because of the love we have, not because of some greater love we hope to attain. So, yes, growing in faith, being a person of prayer, studying the scriptures, and being a good neighbor are all wonderful, important, and even necessary things. It's what we do in the family of God. But if you sometimes struggle to live out these ideals, like any child in any family, are you any less loved by your Heavenly Father? Absolutely not! And if you desire to grow in these things, the best way to go about it is *not* to fear the rejection of God. Growth motivated by fear is no growth at all and would sadden the heart of any parent. And certainly brings no pleasure to God.[3]

The path toward healthy growth begins by reacquainting yourself with God's love. Turn your attention away from your failures and all that you should do and refocus instead on the character of God as put on display in the person and work of Jesus. Hear again that all mercy is yours because of the cross. Ponder the empty tomb and know that Christ walked from it for you: your death's been defeated.

[3] "There is no fear in love, but perfect love casts out fear. For fear has to do with punishment, and whoever fears has not been perfected in love." (1 John 4:18) The work of Jesus makes us confident of God's love, despite our continued struggles. If we are living in fear of God's punishment, the antidote is not to try harder to please him but to return to the promise that in Christ we are already fully loved by him. This then inspires us toward obedience, not as a way to *appease* but out of *gratitude*.

Remember the promise of your baptism: that you are *chosen* by God, *alive* to God, *filled* with the Spirit of God, and *covered* as with a garment in the grace of God. Focus on *that*. Ruminate on *that*. Go to church and celebrate *that*. And then—thoroughly overwhelmed by what you already have—return to the question of "What shall I become?" And watch as the growth God urges begins to emerge in you. Very slowly and imperfectly, for sure. But it will emerge, nonetheless.

Oblivious Children

I am convinced that one of the many reasons we get so caught up in the notion of measuring and climbing (and perversely connecting it to our standing with God) is that we—like typical children—so easily lose sight of the blessings we already possess. The blessings of God become so commonplace to us that we overlook them and then wrongly assume that we are somehow deprived of them.

Think back to when you were fifteen years old. If you were anything like the typical teenager, nothing was ever quite good enough for you. Your parents were not as understanding as you'd like them to be, your house wasn't as big as it could be, your clothes weren't as cool as they could be. It's as though all the hormones raging through your body managed to blind you, keeping you from appreciating all that you possessed. You simply couldn't grasp the grace and goodness that existed in your home. And when Mom or Dad tried to enlighten you about the many blessings you enjoyed, they were met with an epic eye roll followed by, "Whatever! You don't even know!" Sound familiar?

Fast forward to when you're twenty-three, done with school, and working hard to make it on your own. And out of nowhere, it hit you:

you had it really good growing up. Immediately, you called up Mom or Dad and said, "I just realized how hard you worked and how much you provided. Thank you!" And then you moved home.

Like teenagers with hormone-induced tunnel vision, we struggle to see the blessings we already possess. We so quickly lose sight of the truth that those who have faith in Jesus Christ have *already arrived*. We live, right now, at the summit of God's love and grace. The only mountains that exist to climb are ones of our own making. And they carry labels like health and fitness, financial freedom, peer recognition, successful children—you get the idea. The mountains are many, and the range is large. And though many of the mountains are noble, they serve mostly as distractions. We spiritualize these pursuits by convincing ourselves that they are birthrights of the baptized, gifts that God *must* want for his children. And then we spend far too much time with ruler in hand, measuring our progress and wondering why God has to make it so hard or why he hasn't just hoisted us to the top.

It's All Yours

Later in Galatians, Paul reminds the confused church that their status and all of God's blessings have already been secured for them. There's nothing to strive for that hasn't already been won in the cross of Jesus Christ:

> Christ redeemed us from the curse of the law by becoming a curse for us—for it is written, "Cursed is everyone who is hanged on a tree"—so that in Christ Jesus the blessing of Abraham might come to the Gentiles, so that we might receive the promised Spirit through faith. (Galatians 3:13-14)

Jesus measured out every inch of obedience and labored under its burden perfectly. And then he faced the judgment of the cross—for all of *our* failures—and died sacrificially. In doing so, he broke the "curse of the law" and set us free from performing when it comes to God. And we now have—*you* have—every blessing of being in God's family through faith in Christ.

Even when bad things happen, it's yours. Even though your growth is very much a work in progress, it's yours. Even when you're lacking the treasures atop every other "mountain," it's yours. Even when you fail to appreciate it, it's yours. Even when you screw up and show yourself to be a terrible sinner, it's yours. Even when everyone else says, "Do more," it's still yours. Toss the ruler in the trash and hold tight to these words: You have his favor. He calls you his own. You possess all that God has to give.

Rock Bottom

All that being said, there is *one* place where God likes to make himself known in surprising and powerful ways: at rock bottom. You know the place that I'm talking about, right? It's not just when something bad happens; it's more than that. It's when all your energy is spent, your ideas have failed, your future seems bleak, and your life feels like a bust. This is where God loves to show up. But to be honest, it's not that he shows up in new ways at rock bottom but that we are able to see him with greater clarity.

Think again about the metaphor of father and child. Consider the moments of unexpected but relatively harmless pain, like falling off your bike just after you said goodbye to training wheels or taking a poorly thrown baseball to the face in Little League. As a child, in those moments of hurt and pain, we instinctively do two things: we lift our eyes to look for Mom or Dad, and we call their name. Almost without fail, they come running to swoop us up and tell us it's going to be okay. Or, in the case of my dad, to yell from the stands, "Walk it off, bud! A bruise can't kill ya!" The point being that, prior to the moment of pain, we were rather oblivious to their presence—riding carefree up and down the block or picking dandelions in the outfield. But at the moment pain and helplessness overwhelmed us, our awareness of Mom and Dad returned with a vengeance, and they came running. Our relationship with God works much the same way.

As we've been learning, God is not tucked away at the top of some metaphorical mountain. He is with us. Right now. But so very often we are oblivious to his presence and blind to his goodness. Yet, when failure, sickness, or some kind of struggle knocks us in the nose, it's then that our distractions dissolve and the facade of our self-sufficiency is broken. We see ourselves clearly, as children in need of their Father's help. And so, we cry out from rock bottom, and he comes running. It's then that we remember just how close and how incredibly compassionate our God is. But don't be fooled; it often takes a fly ball to the face to figure it out.

The apostle Paul understood this. In his letter to the church in Corinth, he writes, "If I must boast, I will boast of the things that show my weakness" (2 Corinthians 11:30). Is Paul proud of his problems? No; he's proud of what his problems, his weaknesses, have reminded him of. He's grateful for the gift of seeing God's immense grace with the clear eyes that pain provides. Hold that insight in your back pocket and save it for the next time life falls apart. And there will be a next time. The temptation will be to keep your eyes closed and tell yourself that you've slid down the side of whatever mountain you were trying to scale. "God is further now than he's ever been," you'll think. But according to Paul, the opposite is true. When you're at your lowest point, you are most ready to realize God's love.

Being a pastor, I often have the opportunity to sit with people who are at rock bottom. Almost inevitably, as I invite them to pray, they'll say some version of the following: "God feels so far away." To which I'll gently respond, "He's here right now. And he's doing what he always does: loving the sinner, showing mercy to those who are messed up. He's here, right now, with you and me. And today, though it's difficult, we have the good fortune of getting to see him at work."

Open your Eyes

Despite all that's been said, you may still be struggling to see how God is present in your life. It may still seem as though he's far away, holding out on you, or off on top of some far-away mountain you need to climb. If (and when) you feel that way, my encouragement for you is simple: open your eyes.

Since the beginning of the Christian faith, followers of Jesus have maintained that God generously makes himself known in three ways. When we are tied up in the lie that God needs to be chased down, sought out, or won over, all we need to do is open our eyes to the places all around us where he promises to be present.

First, open your eyes to creation. The next time God feels far away, I encourage you to go for a walk. The beauty, the complexity of the created world, calls us out of ourselves and forces us to ponder the existence of God. When life gets difficult, the last thing you need is to continue to sit in your apartment and stare at your phone. It's helpful, if not necessary, to get out and see the beauty of what God has made. Doing so has a way of reminding us of his power and his presence. Staring at a tall tree or just taking in the smile of a stranger sends a message to our hearts and minds: "He's not far off. He's surrounded me with all of this beauty." Even the most ardent atheist would admit that, at some point, the glory of the world we live in—as witnessed on the shores of the Pacific Ocean at sunset or standing at the rim of the Grand Canyon—has caused them to question the existence of a creator. That's what the wonders of this world do; they turn our hearts toward heaven.

Of course, creation is limited in what it can tell us about God. The beauty of this world speaks of God's presence, for sure, but it does so with incomplete language. It speaks of God in generalities. You can't uproot a redwood tree, turn it over, and see the words "Made by Jesus" on the bottom. And the stars don't align to spell out his promises in the night sky. For greater detail, we need to keep our eyes open, looking now to his people.

If you want to feel the presence of God in a truly tangible way, open your eyes to his people and make yourself comfortable in his church. I write this fully understanding that you may not be a fan of the church. The one you grew up in may have felt a bit backward and old-fashioned—if you grew up in church at all. And it may seem to you that churches are filled with more than a few people who like to rail about the sins of others while often paying little attention to their own. Not to mention the fact that church people fail to measure up to current social standards of influence and have earned very little cultural acclaim. Or, to use words my teenage daughter would appreciate, "Our swag game is weak." There's no getting around the fact that the church is a collection of terribly messed up people, doing strange things when they gather[4] and holding tight to counter-cultural truths. And yet, it's within this seemingly out-of-step, imperfect, and insignificant community that God is profoundly active.

By virtue of their baptisms, followers of Jesus carry within themselves the Holy Spirit of God. The church—gathered together on a Sunday or scattered as individuals throughout the week—takes God with them at all times. God promises that their presence is always an extension of *his* presence.

Do you grasp what this means? Even though it is wrapped in human flesh and hidden in human foibles, every hug from the baptized, every word of encouragement, every text message, every conversation over coffee, every awkward potluck in a church basement carries with it an encounter with God. The church is the body of Christ, and therefore, every encounter with the church is an encounter with God. At times, people will say that they wished God would just show up or that they long for some kind of tangible, personal encounter. Open your eyes. When a pastor stands in front of the church and tells you you're forgiven, it's God speaking to you. When the nice old lady at

---

[4] Christian worship is inherently other-worldly. It reflects the values of a different kingdom, it has practices commanded by a God that so many have never met, and it betrays a hope that no one, apart from those who have faith in Christ, possesses. The singing of songs, the confession of sins, the proclamation of God's love, the reciting of creeds, and the celebration of baptism and the Lord's Supper are objectively strange to the outsider and the uninitiated. It's beautiful in its own way, but otherworldly and strange for sure. Any effort to remove this strangeness would result in something other than Christian worship. However, every effort should be made to make corporate Christian worship understandable to outsiders. They must be able to grasp what's happening so that they might themselves be stirred to belief through what's taking place.

church tells you that she's praying for you, it's God encouraging you. When a friend in faith speaks a tough biblical truth to you, it's God correcting you. When the people of Jesus pack the pews all around you, it's God drawing near to you.

But there's more. The most powerful of places that God is present is in his Word. We will dive into this in much more detail in chapter five, but of all the places to look for God's presence, this is the most important. The Word of God is so much more than the Bible or the story of what God has done for the world in Jesus Christ. What Christians believe is that God's Word—*written* in the pages of scripture, *proclaimed* on the lips of the baptized, and *made flesh* in the person of Jesus—provides a transformative encounter with God.

The Word of God is the power behind baptism, turning it from some ritual with water to a new birth into God's family. It's what makes a meal of bread and wine, which one might otherwise see as a time to merely reflect on the love of Jesus, into a feast where the food is the actual sin-forgiving and faith-strengthening body and blood of Jesus. It's where we learn the details about God—who he is, how he loves us, all he's done to save us—and the specifics about ourselves, most importantly of our desperate need for grace. And these words *do* something to us. They change us. They stir up sorrow over our struggle to know and love God, and they create a saving faith in the person and in the promises of Jesus Christ. The Word of God is not just information; it is power, it is a divine encounter. It provides—for those who look for it and listen to it—a transformation.

Open your eyes to the presence and power of God that is all around you. He is not far from any of us. There is overwhelming evidence for—and opportunity to experience—his presence woven into the mundane realities of everyday life. Even yours.

Look around at his creation. Reach out to his people. Hear his Word.

Easy: It's Grace

The story is told[5] of a conference of religious scholars that took place many years ago. The topic was "comparative religion." At the gathering, a debate emerged about the uniqueness of Christianity. Some argued that what set the Christian faith apart was the incarnation. "No," replied some of the scholars present, "there are other traditions with similar teachings." Others asserted that the doctrine of the resurrection of the dead on the last day was the great differentiator. "No," shouted one of the participants, "Judaism and Islam also teach that there will be a resurrection of all flesh."

It was at this point in the discussion that C.S. Lewis, the author and theologian, walked into the auditorium. I'm sure he looked every bit the part of the crazy professor, complete with tweed jacket, stacks of papers, and a distant, distracted look on his face. The noise of the debate aroused his attention. "What's this all about?" he asked.

"We are debating the uniqueness of Christianity," shared one of his colleagues.

"That's easy," said Lewis as he rolled his eyes. The room settled into a quiet hum of conversation, waiting for Lewis to elaborate. Realizing

---

[5] The story, relayed by Philip Yancey in *What's So Amazing About Grace*, is likely apocryphal and for my purposes has been embellished. True or not, the point made is accurate. Grace, while not the sole differentiator of Christianity from other religious traditions, is the greatest.

they wanted more, he looked up from his papers and surveyed the conference.

"It's grace," Lewis said. And then he walked out, having satisfied the question and stunned his colleagues.

It really is that simple. The Christian gospel proclaims to tired bodies, anxious minds, and hearts made heavy by sin that God gives forgiveness and new life to weary, incapable, and unworthy people. And he requires nothing in advance or in return. No bloody hands, no busy feet—*nothing*. It's just grace.

There is no karma to avoid or contract for us to keep. As Bono, lead singer of U2 put it,[6] "The love of God (in Jesus Christ) has interrupted the consequences for our actions." And we just get to enjoy God's love and all that his son has won for the world.

Because of Jesus, there is no mountain to climb or progress to measure in order to get right with or get more from God. By faith, we are carried to the top of a mountain called Mercy. And up here, all that he has to offer is ours.

I know, it sounds too easy. Too simple. I know it's contrary to everything you've been taught about how the world works. And you know what? You're right. It *is* easy. It *is* simple. It *is* counter-intuitive. But that doesn't make it wrong.

That's what makes it grace.

Taking Inventory

Grace, an undeserved and unearned favor from God, is the foundation for a sustainable and truly joyful spiritual life. Anything else burdens

---

[6] Quoted from *Bono: In Conversation with Michka Assayas* (Riverhead Books).

the soul, likely to the degree that things like peace and hope will feel like impossible ideas, rather than ever-present realities.

And yet, our junk drawers remain filled with items that encourage us to indulge the worst of our religious impulses, to lean deeply on our ability to manufacture our own sense of meaning, and to provide our own peace. The pre-eminent example of this might just be what we—particularly in the West—do with work. It's one of the most insidious, and intoxicating, of our idols (a term we will expound in a later chapter). And any serious attempt to deconstruct unhealthy religious ideas, must confront the habit we have of turning desks into deities, of making one's 9-to-5 into a means of salvation.

QUESTIONS TO CONSIDER:

When have you felt the closest to God? What was the circumstance surrounding that sensation and how would you describe that feeling to others?

In times of difficulty and struggle, where do you go, spiritually? Do you get angry with God, or do you blame yourself?

How open are you to the idea that our performance, and our circumstances, have no bearing on our proximity to God and his attitude toward us?

FOUR

The Why of Work

Bob: "Looks like you've been missing a lot of work lately."
Peter: "I wouldn't say I've been missing it, Bob."

—OFFICE SPACE

I'VE GOT TWO WORDS for you: Monday morning.

Those two words are powerful, aren't they? They stir up emotion; they elicit a response. When we think about the alarm going off on our phone, rolling out of bed, and heading back to work after a nice, relaxing weekend, something happens inside us.

Some of us are filled with excitement and anticipation when Monday rolls around. We love our work and feel most alive when we are grinding hard at the office or on the job site. The work we do gives us life, and Mondays mean jumping back into something satisfying.

Others feel like Monday (and every work day) is something we have to get through to survive. We loathe our work and struggle not to feel stuck in it or as though a piece of us is dying as we do it. It feels like our life is being slowly drained with every notification we respond to on Slack or every passenger who hails us on Uber. We count the seconds to when we can log off the computer in our home office or grab our coat and kiss the cubicle goodbye for the weekend.

And then there are those who just endure Monday. We don't love our work; we don't hate our work. We just put up with it. It's one of many things in life that, whether you like it or not, must be done. So, each day you step into the classroom, you jump into the Zoom call, or you throw on the apron and you work. But it's a means to an end. You work so that the car note can be paid, you can chip away at your student loans, your daughter can have a cell phone, and your son can play club soccer.

But what if I told you that there can be more to Mondays—much more—than whatever emotion overtakes you each time the alarm goes off?

One of the more practical and profound implications of the Christian faith is that it transforms our understanding of human labor for the better. Whatever it is that you do for a living, when viewed through the lens of God's Word, is infused with immense purpose and lasting peace. And it's not just the things you do for a paycheck but all your labor in life. Every hat you wear, every responsibility you carry, is reborn when understood in light of Jesus, of what he's worked for and won for you in his death and resurrection.

The ID Badge

It's right at the top of the drawer. It needs to be easy to access—after all, you wear it every day. Printed on the front is a picture of you that you don't particularly care for. You weren't feeling very cute that first day in the office when they snapped your photo. It has your name, properly spelled for a change, and a unique number assigned to you in the organization. On the back is some kind of barcode that gets scanned each time you enter and exit your office building. They say it's for security, but you're certain they're keeping copious notes about how much time you spend hiding in your car listening to true-crime podcasts while you eat your lunch.

This ID badge is not just something you wear at work; it's symbolic of your work. It represents the fact that the bulk of the hours afforded to you each day, a majority of the days in each and every week, and a significant portion of your life overall, is dedicated to doing a certain set of tasks. Wearing the ID badge is fitting, not just because the employee manual says that you have to, but because that which we spend so much of our lives doing becomes inextricably tied, or so it seems, to how we perceive ourselves, how we measure the meaning of our lives and our worth in this world. As such, our labor—whether we love it or loathe it—becomes a religion of sorts for us. We sacrifice the best of our years for it, offer our treasures of time and talent to it, and seek in return the blessing of meaning and knowing we matter.

And why wouldn't we? To give so much of yourself to something for so long—especially something that, at times, can feel so very dull or be so deeply draining—for no greater purpose would be such a waste, wouldn't it? For many, if not most, donning the ID badge (or throwing on the uniform, logging onto the computer, checking email, doing the laundry, chasing the kids) becomes an act of worship. It's your offering to a god that demands your all in the hopes that it will bless you back with something greater and deeper than what we can conjure on our own.

Worshiping Work

The truth is that desks make terrible deities. To put it another way, even the best job is a bad god. Some will say that the world has become less religious. That's not true. Yes, the world, especially in the West, is less *traditionally* religious. Church attendance in the United States has been on a steep and steady decline for decades, and more people identify as religious "nones" than ever before.[1] But as the great poet Bob Dylan sang, "You gotta serve somebody." Everyone has someone, something they look to in order to help provide a feeling of self-worth, a sense of purpose, greater meaning, and—perhaps most of all—a way to make sense of and avoid pain. We will cover this in great detail in chapter eight, but whatever that thing is for you, whether it's Jesus, the Buddha, the acquisition of wealth, the wellbeing of your kids, or the applause of your peers, this is, by definition, your deity. It is what you fear, love, and trust above all things and, as such, is your functional savior. It's what you worship. It's your god. In our increasingly secular society, it's not that fewer and fewer worship a god but that they are forgoing the traditional ones. And for many, the new god of choice is work.

In a study on the epidemic of teenage anxiety, Pew Research found that ninety-five percent of teens stated that "finding a job they love" was very important to finding meaning as an adult. They ranked it higher than "kindness to others," "starting a family," and "having a vibrant faith." Let that sink in. For nearly *all* of the teenagers surveyed, finding the right job beat out compassion, relationships, and religion

---

[1] Gregory A. Smith, "About Three-in-Ten U.S. Adults Are Now Religiously Unaffiliated." Pew Research Center's Religion; Public Life Project. Pew Research Center, April 14, 2022. https://www.pewresearch.org/religion/2021/12/14/about-three-in-ten-u-s-adults-are-now-religiously-unaffiliated/.

as a key element in their thriving as an adult.[2] We hear this belief reflected in the language used surrounding work—not just by young adults but by virtually everyone. We are told we have to hustle for our dreams, that we must pursue our passions, maximize our impact, and crush our goals. And the passions we are pursuing, the goals we are crushing, the impact we are after, are almost always lived out in the arena of work and career.

To be clear, finding a job that you love is not wrong. As one who loves his work, I can attest to the fact that laboring away at work you find meaningful and fulfilling, while also taking home a paycheck, is delightful. I highly recommend it. Work is not a bad thing; it's a very good thing. But we must be wise. When we speak this way about work, when we place such massive existential expectations on our work, we are coming dangerously close to making an idol out of it. We are trying to get from our "nine-to-five" what we used to seek from the 9 a.m. service on Sunday morning. And what so many of us are learning the hard way is that when work is worshiped, it leaves you exhausted and anxious, depleted physically and empty spiritually.

When work is worshiped as a god, you quickly discover that the god you're serving is never satisfied. You never arrive in the Promised Land. There's always more to do. Think about it: the most common job in the United States is a cashier.[3] It's a perfectly respectable and

---

[2] Juliana Menasce Horowitz and Nikki Graf, "Most U.S. Teens See Anxiety, Depression as Major Problems." Pew Research Center's Social & Demographic Trends Project. February 20, 2019. https://www.pewresearch.org/social-trends/2019/02/20/most-u-s-teens-see-anxiety-and-depression-as-a-major-problem-among-their-peers/.

[3] Based on data from the U.S. Bureau of Labor Statistics, more than four million Americans work in retail sales with an average pay of just over $13 an hour.

much-needed job. Yet, my guess is that few would say that working the checkout lane at the grocery store is their dream job connected to their personal passion or a prime source of their sense of worth in this world. Still, in our work-worshiping world, that's precisely the pressure put on the guy sliding your cereal across the scanner. So, what happens to him? Does he wrestle with deep discontent, longing to "do something else"? And what about when he does land the more ideal gig? He will be met with the fact that even dream jobs have dull days and that you must relentlessly produce and continually earn your keep to remain in the dream role. The discontent that got him the ideal work can quickly turn to disillusionment once he's landed it. And before long he finds himself caught in what feels like a meaningless cycle. A cycle encapsulated perfectly by Edward Norton's character in the 1999 film *Fight Club*, which is itself derived from a 1928 column by syndicated humorist Robert Quillen and has been stolen, spoken, and shared by countless others, because of how deeply it resonates with the American worker: "We work jobs we hate, so we can spend money we don't have on shit we don't need, to impress people we don't like."

More than anything, desks make terrible deities because they cannot deliver to you what you demand from them. Instead, they just keep demanding that you deliver. Desks make terrible deities because what you end up discovering is that there is no grace for you in your pursuit of meaning and purpose as you push more paper, serve more clients, or preach better sermons. Your work will

(U.S. BUREAU OF LABOR STATISTICS. 2021. "May 2021 National Occupational Employment and Wage Estimates." Bls.gov. https://www.bls.gov/oes/current/oes _nat.htm.)

not sacrifice anything for you. It will not die for you. Instead, it will insist that, in order to derive the peace, meaning, and purpose you long for, you must be willing to die for it. You must die at the desk. With this dynamic at play, is it any wonder that American workers are being diagnosed with higher rates of anxiety and depression than ever before?[4]

Do the ups and downs, pushes and pulls, the doldrums and difficulties of work feel like more than a source of simple stress and manageable annoyances? Do the pressures to thrive, to succeed, to achieve and accomplish feel like an existential life or death weight on your shoulders? Do you rationalize a failure to spend time with your family, to nurture your spirituality, or to care for your physical health by saying, "When I hit the next sales goal, finish this project, or hit six figures, *then* I'll change my priorities"? Do you find that, when you reflect on your work, you often end up questioning your talent or the career choices you've made or drifting into a mild depression? If so, then you might just be guilty—like so very many of us—of making your desk your deity. You've made work your god.

Wear a Mask

Straight out of the gate in the Book of Genesis, God tells us that we were made to work. He designed us for lives of labor. Before there was any sign of sin, before anything was corrupted, before there was

---

[4] A recent study found that two-thirds of employees have clinically measurable symptoms of anxiety or depression. ("Many US Workers Suffer from Depression or Anxiety but Their Employers Are Unaware." Baton Rouge Business Report. September 21, 2021.) https://www.businessreport.com/business/many-us-workers -suffer-from-depression-or-anxiety-but-their-employers-are-unaware.

anything awful whatsoever in the world, there was work to do. "The Lord God took the man and put him in the garden of Eden to work it and keep it" (Genesis 2:15). Work is one of the many gifts given by God to humankind. In fact, studies show that the need to take part in productive labor is so hard-wired into humanity that long-term unemployment may be more damaging to one's mental health than the sudden loss of a loved one.[5] We were, indeed, made for it. But that's very different from believing that work *makes us*. As I said earlier, your job is a terrible god. And yet, it's important to grasp that work itself is *of God*. It is divine in origin. Grasping that truth is critical if you're to rightly understand and enjoy your work.

When my son was little, I asked him a question: "Who makes everything?"

He thought for a moment and then said, "Mommy!"

I let out a laugh before setting him straight. "No, son. Mommy *does* everything. God is the one who makes everything."

All that we see and experience comes from God. This is why, when good things happen, people of faith offer him thanks and praise. It's also why, when bad things happen, we look to the heavens and ask him, "Why?!" This is also why, when we need anything—from a cure to our cancer to a calm night with the kids after a tough day at the office—we reach out to him. We cry out in prayer and we ask him to help. Jesus himself encouraged this when he said, "Pray like this: Heavenly Father ... give us this day our daily bread" (Matthew 6:11). God is the giver of all good things. We are dependent upon

[5] Megan McArdle, "Unemployment: A Fate Worse than Death." *Time*, 19 Feb. 2014, time.com/9009/unemployment-is-worse-than-death/. Accessed 15 June 2022.

him for everything. But let me ask you this: how does God deliver the bread? How does he care for the cancer patient? How does he keep you entertained and relaxed on a Friday night after the kids have passed out?

God delivers gifts *to* people *through* people. He uses you and me in our various professions as a means of answering prayers and providing for our every need. Sure, he could just make bread magically appear on our table. And if you stop to think about it, it is kind of magical. When you consider the very long chain of events—people, processes, and technology—that culminated in your being able to tap your phone and have whole wheat bagels delivered to your doorstep, it's a bit mind-blowing. God works through farmers and bakers, through those who stock the shelves at your grocery store, paying off student loans through side hustles on DoorDash to keep you fed. He works through the showrunners on your favorite HBO series to keep you entertained. He uses phlebotomists and lab technicians to inform you that your thyroid is working properly and that a multivitamin would serve you well. He uses UPS drivers to keep you stocked with stuff from Amazon and the guy who grabs your trash on Tuesdays and Saturdays to keep your backyard from becoming a landfill.

Martin Luther, the sixteenth-century reformer, once wrote:

What else is all our work to God—whether in the fields, in the garden, in the city, in the house, in war, or in government—but just such a child's performance, by which he wants to give his gifts in the fields, at home, and everywhere else? These are the masks of God, behind which he wants to remain concealed and do all things ... Labor, and let him give the fruits.

Govern, and let him give his blessing. Fight, and let him give the victory. Preach, and let him win hearts. Take a husband or a wife, and let him produce the children. Eat and drink, and let him nourish and strengthen you. And so on. In all our doings he is to work through us, and he alone shall have the glory from it ....[6]

Your work is a mask of God. We are children at play, behind whom our Heavenly Father is hidden and through whom he is at work. And he's at work through you, regardless of whether you recognize it or believe in him. It's not as though he's only involved in the labor of the faith-filled churchgoer. No; as the old hymn says, "This is my Father's world." All of it. All of us. Whether you're a devout Christian dentist or an agnostic orthodontist, God is hidden behind your work, using you to fill cavities and straighten teeth.

This truth, if you ponder the implications and allow it to sink in, is life-changing. Your work is not only "of God" in the sense that he's created us for it and commanded us to do it, but also because the God of the Universe chooses to deliver necessary and needed gifts through you as you do it. Your labor is part of God's grand plan of provision. Have you considered that? You are God's means for meeting someone else's needs. Your work is God's answer to someone else's prayer. This truth instills our labor with the highest of purpose while at the same time keeping us grounded and humble. God is at work, so we treat it with seriousness and find great meaning in it. But it is *God* who is at work; he's called us to it, and he is the one who makes possible any and all fruit that flows from it. As Luther said, "[He] alone shall

[6] Luther's Works, vol. 14, p. 114-115.

have the glory from it ..." It's a bit more difficult to worship our work when we focus on who actually deserves the credit for it.

Measured in Love

As is the case with so many of the misconceptions we find in our spiritual junk drawers, getting things right will require us to talk about love. Much of our spiritual dysfunction is due to a confusion of love or, as Augustine would put it, a "disordering" of our love. We love good things in the wrong way, in the wrong order, and for the wrong reasons. This is certainly true of our warped relationship with work. Jesus lays it out rather simply for us:

> You shall love the Lord your God with all your heart and with all your soul and with all your mind. This is the great and first commandment. And a second is like it: You shall love your neighbor as yourself. On these two commandments depend all the law and the prophets. (Matthew 22:37–40)

The meaning of life, the point and purpose of all labor, is love. But notice, it's not love of self. First, it's love for God. Second, it's love for your neighbor. We can't correctly understand the rest of God's revelation unless we first wrap our warped hearts around this truth.

Love is the "why" of your work. It doesn't matter what you do. If you're launching the next great tech start-up, it's supposed to be about love. If you're a stay-at-home dad, you fold the laundry and make lunches out of love. If you're a pilot, you land the plane safely out of love. If you're a member of Congress, you're sent there to legislate with love. If you're the guy who shows up at my house four times a year to spray for bugs, it's an act of love—it's not so loving to the cockroaches we're trying to keep out of our hallway bathroom, but my daughter sure does appreciate it. Like so many other things in this world that God has designed, we get work "right" when we realize that, although we are involved in it, we are not the ones being served by it. It doesn't exist to prop up our self-worth or earn us acceptance. Our labor is about loving others.

This is the key to finding satisfaction in your work: draw a line between what you do and how it blesses and benefits your neighbor. Can you see how the work you're doing—in the office, at home, volunteering at church, or being active in your community—is essential to a system through which God is protecting, providing, helping, entertaining, or encouraging someone else? Sure, it may be that your contribution feels like a very small piece of the puzzle, but can you see how your piece completes the whole of a work of love God is offering to someone else? Are you able to grasp how, by making change at the register or correcting code in some new piece of software, watching grandkids, or mowing lawns, you are giving a gift to someone else? Can you draw the line of love back to someone else?

In our idolatry of work, we will put pressure on ourselves to do work that "changes the world." We think that unless masses of people are affected by it or recognize it, it is somehow secondary or falls short. But can you see how arrogant and self-defeating of an idea that is? The truth is that few of us, an incredibly small number of humans, will have the opportunity to affect change on a global scale or even across a particular industry. And few will do work that gets the applause of a crowd or the massive recognition of their peers. But when love is the litmus test of vocational success, all of us can thrive. Each of us, regardless of the scope of our impact, has the same high calling to bring blessing, answered prayers, and "daily bread" to a whole bunch of little worlds. And then, together, God uses our contribution to serve, shape, and care for the whole.

As a child of the 1980s, I grew up a fan of old-school NBA—you know, back when you could hand-check your opponent and throw an elbow at the guy trying to drive the lane without getting tossed from the game. My basketball teeth were cut on the Bad Boy Detroit Pistons, Larry Bird's Celtics, Magic's Lakers, and Jordan's ascendance as the greatest of all time with the Chicago Bulls. In March of 1990, Michael Jordan put on one of the best performances the NBA has ever seen. I remember it. I was ten years old. He scored sixty-nine points against the Cleveland Cavaliers. A rookie on that Bulls team named Stacy King played just seventeen minutes and scored only one point. After the game, King was asked by reporters to reflect on the history that had been made that night. King's response was this: "I'll always remember this as the night Michael Jordan and I combined to score seventy points." It's funny, but it's also profound. The rookie chose to frame his work, his contribution to the game, as part of something greater. It wasn't just one point—that single point was part of a record-setting night and an overtime win.

That is how we are to see our work. God is using our labor of love, no matter how small or mundane it might seem, as part of a much greater gift of love that he's offering the world. Sure, you can say, "I just bake bread. I'm nothing but a girl in a bakery, waking up way too early, rolling out dough, and getting covered in flour." Or, when asked what you do for a living, you could take a cue from Stacey King: "I'm not just a baker; I partner with God to feed the world."

That said, it may be that no matter how hard you try you can't connect the dots between the work that you do and love for your neighbor. You just can't see how it's a tangible blessing to someone else. If that's the case then it might be time to find something else to do. You should seek out work in which it's easy to find and appreciate the line between your labor and loving others. More often than not that line does exist, we are just easily blind to it. And if you're struggling in this regard, rather than trade in one ID badge for another, you should pray for your eyes to be opened and to see how you are already in partnership with God, to see that he's hidden behind our work.

Can you see it in the work that you do?

Can you draw a line between your labor and how it helps your neighbor?

Freed by Jesus

If you're like most people, then all of this talk about living and working for others sounds great but also makes you a bit nervous. The nervousness comes from an understandable concern that our own needs might be overlooked in it all. The truth is that no matter how altruistically we try to spin it, we have some deep, personal needs that we bring to our daily labors. Beyond paying the bills, we rely on our work to make sense of and add meaning to our lives. If we live to love others, do we run the risk of depriving ourselves in the process? This is where Jesus comes in.

We are set free to see our work as an adventure in loving others and not merely a means for propping up our egos or proving our worth. We are free to live our lives in love for others because he has given his life in love for us. Our deepest needs—to matter, to have meaning, to be known and seen and so much more—are all met in him. What you need to flourish and thrive has been won for you, earned, and given to you in Jesus Christ. Specifically, he's secured your approval and acceptance in the eyes of God the Father. And by connecting you to the Father, to your Creator, you now have the ability to see and appreciate the fact that your work (your whole life!) is part of something much bigger, something meaningful and eternal. And by virtue of Jesus's death and resurrection, all your sins are forgiven and the power stolen from the sources of your shame. They have no claim over you, meaning that you no longer have to be driven by guilt or motivated by a desire to cover past failures with professional accolades. Instead, you can dive into the tasks of the day knowing that in the things that matter most, you've arrived. Because of Jesus Christ, you are freed to work *from* a love and acceptance you already possess rather than *for* a love and acceptance you're trying to earn.

And all of this—acceptance in the eyes of the Father, awareness that your work is part of his plan, the forgiveness of sin, freedom from shame—is given to you as a free gift. It's been won for the world by Jesus and belongs to those baptized into his name. Unlike your paycheck, it is completely unearned. You don't have to die at your desk to enjoy it. Jesus died and rose to procure it. He did all the work. By grace through faith in him alone, we simply receive it and enjoy it. It's yours, right now. You are not and you will not be deprived as you live this life of love. Your deepest needs are met in the person and work of Jesus.

Can you sense how this takes the pressure off your work? Sure, as we've discussed, the fact that God is hidden in our work adds great meaning and purpose to it. But at the same time, if all this is true, then it frees us to see our work as just that: work. Important? Yes. Necessary for my neighbor? A hundred percent. Divine in design? Absolutely. But is it a means for attaining lasting peace and proving my worth in this world? Is it riddled with so much existential urgency? No. Jesus has done the work that gives us worth and provides us peace. Our work, while important, is still just work. The pressure is off, and now freedom abounds.

One might think that such a view would encourage laziness in our labor. If work isn't our god, then why give it our best effort? But in fact, the opposite is true. With the pressure that comes with making work your idol now off the table, we are freer than ever to bring our best to it. Think about it: if Jesus has done the work that truly matters and given us the spoils, then we are free to bring a spirit of risk, innovation, and adventure to our work because even if we fail, we will be fine. Christ has secured our future.

We are free to have healthy boundaries when it comes to our work. We can leave work at work and be more present at home. Because if work can't save us, and Jesus already has, then it makes no sense to work in a way that undermines our most important relationships. It gains us nothing we don't already have in Christ. So, do your best, and then, when the time comes, remember that in Christ you're free to enjoy your family and find time to rest.

It also frees us to treat those we work for and alongside with greater dignity. We are no longer incentivized to objectify others, treating them as a means to the end of our own "salvation." Instead, we can see them as people we are called to love and serve for their benefit, in and through our work. If Jesus has served us in his work, then we are free to serve others in ours.

Our feelings of nervousness and any concerns of laziness are ultimately unfounded. Hang that ID badge around your neck, knowing that as you do, your deepest needs are met and that there is a joyful, meaningful mission in front of you. Those truths lead you to walk through your day with peace in regard to your own well-being and to work with excellence, doing whatever faithfulness requires.

Clipping Thorns

Tim was a fixture in my church growing up. My memories of him are of being greeted with bear hugs, high fives, and conversations about professional wrestling every time I strolled into the sanctuary on a Sunday morning. Tim loved wrestling. His favorite wrestler was a character known as The Undertaker, of whom he did a spot-on (and hilarious) impression. Tim had Down Syndrome. And while it meant he faced some hurdles and some limitations in life, it mostly served to make him one of the kindest, most authentically loving people I've ever known.

I remember the first time I ever encountered Tim outside of church. I was a senior in high school and had walked into the local flower shop in my small mid-Michigan town to buy flowers for my girlfriend. Glancing over the owner's shoulder as he rang up my purchase, I noticed a familiar smile emanating from the back where the arrangements were being prepared. It was Tim. Our eyes met, and he came running from the back of the shop to offer me the usual bear hug and high five. He then dragged me by the arm and led me to his workspace.

Tim had a simple but important job. For a few hours every day, he would trim flowers. But his specialty was removing thorns from roses. He was incredibly proud and very excited to show me his work, more excited than he even got about wrestling (and did I mention that he really loved wrestling?). He showed me the tools he used and asked me to watch as he carefully removed each thorn from the flowers that I'd be giving to Lisa. At the end of the tour, Tim gave me a giant hug, buried his face in my shoulder, and said, "I love you, man!"

Prior to our encounter at the flower shop I had never imagined Tim with a job. He was always just the joyful guy at church. And if you'd asked me, I would have told you that a job for Tim was probably not possible, given my ignorance and assumptions about his abilities. I saw him as someone who, while funny and loving, likely needed more service from others than he could provide to them. It had never crossed my mind that Tim would be serving and supporting me in any way. And yet, there he was, trimming flowers—the flowers I would give to my girlfriend, who would later become my wife. Those flowers that served as a small token of my love, that were a symbol of my desire to be more than some high school crush, were prepared and made perfect by my wrestling-loving friend from church. Lisa was able to grasp them tight and appreciate my sentiment—without feeling a sting and noticing nothing but the beauty of her favorite flower—because Tim had trimmed the thorns.

That day it struck me: God employs us all. No matter who you are, no matter your age or ability, there is a way for you to love your neighbor. And in such work—whether you're closing million-dollar deals, changing diapers, filing papers, counseling anxious teens, passing laws, or even just trimming flowers—*God* is at work. That's where the joy, peace, and freedom we are so desperately clamoring for in our various callings are truly found.

Despite the incessant messaging of our age, your ID badge can't save you. Your professional accomplishments won't rescue you from the freight train of mortality barreling toward us all or answer the gnawing questions of purpose and meaning that keep us up at night. Your work won't rescue you. But God can, and he has in Jesus Christ. In Christ, the enemies are defeated, the questions are answered, and the victory is given to you. And now, neither your work nor anything else needs to be laden with the pressures of salvation.

You're free to see work rightly: it can't save you, but it can serve others. It won't get you closer to the divine, but it can bring the divine nearer to your neighbor. Those two words, "Monday morning," may never elicit joy. But Mondays can be forever packed with purpose and filled with peace, which makes that terrible alarm a little more tolerable.

Taking Inventory

So far, we've addressed some of the significant, and all-too-common, ways in which the foundation of our spirituality gets built on our own efforts. Technically speaking, we've focused on the faulty soteriology (doctrine of salvation) at the center of dysfunctional religion. While more could be said, we'll now turn toward the more relational aspects of spirituality, which are also rife with misunderstandings and unhelpful assumptions.

It's been said that true religion is not so much a religion at all, but a relationship. Indeed, a key tenet of the historic Christian faith is that God not only exists but that he has a personal nature: he can be spoken to and heard, his presence can be felt, and his truths can be understood. But one's understanding of how all this relating with the divine takes place is critical.

So, does God actually speak? Can we truly hear his voice? And if so, what's his reason behind being so relational?

QUESTIONS TO CONSIDER:

Reflect on the various vocations, or callings, that you have—from a job you are paid to do, to family responsibilities, and any roles that you play in the community. Which of these is the most satisfying for you, and why?

Why is it so easy for one's sense of worth and wellbeing to get wrapped up in their work? Do you ever struggle with this?

Identify the least enjoyable aspects of your various vocations. Despite the difficulties, are you able to articulate the gifts that God is giving to your neighbor through these efforts? If so, who are the "neighbors" being served and what are they receiving?

How God Speaks

"I read the Bible every day."

—DENZEL WASHINGTON

I SWEAR, I PERSONALLY have sixteen different pairs. And with every member of our family attached to various screens, we're the proud owners of more EarPods than we know what to do with.

The sleek, bright white (and famously impossible to keep in your ear) headphones used to come packaged with every single iPhone sold. That is until Apple decided to move the world in a wireless direction. With the introduction of the wireless AirPods, headphones ceased to be shipped with new phones. Consumers were forced— excuse me, *encouraged*—to make yet another purchase in order to enjoy optimal audio as they scroll through footage of talking Siberian Huskies on TikTok. The upside? No cords to untangle and no wires shorting out. The downside? The joy of going on a jog and having one pod slip out of your ear, falling to the ground, and bouncing into a storm drain.

It's a good thing you've got more than a dozen backups tied up in knots and stuffed in various drawers in your home. Let's just hope they have the right plug on the end of them. If not, no worries—they sell a dongle (yes, that's the word) for just thirty-five dollars that will make it all work perfectly. But until it arrives, you'll be listening to your workout mix in mono.

The Headphones

Apple's old-school, original EarPods are so ubiquitous that they've even made their way into your spiritual junk drawer. Look closely, and you'll see a white cord woven in and through the heap of other items. Good luck trying to remove them. Pulling on what looks like a loose end will result in lifting nearly every other item out of the drawer too. These headphones might as well be a python wrapped around its prey. There's little chance of it simply letting go; you'll need to resign yourself to a solid fifteen minutes of untying a knot of cord clinging to pencils, paperclips, hair ties, and even a mini screwdriver used to repair your glasses.

The headphones represent the idea that we have the ability to hear from God himself, to listen to his voice. It's a belief intertwined with everything else in our spiritual junk drawers. How (and what) we hear from God shapes—in no small way—what we believe about God. And hearing from God is foundational to faith. The question is this: what are your headphones, so to speak, connected to?

Some believe that hearing from God is a matter of disconnecting from distractions and tuning into a message buried deep in one's own heart or mind. For others, it's about engaging with nature and hearing the voice of God in the rustles of the leaves, stirred by the wind. And for others, it's about discerning signs and signals sent from the Universe and connecting the dots of meaning between otherwise random experiences. For others, hearing from God means devouring the podcast of the latest cultural guru whose insights on how to maximize your potential, rid yourself of shame, and manifest your desires seem utterly divine.

The Christian faith teaches that God is speaking and that you and I can tune in to hear his voice. Not only that, but the historic Christian faith holds to a belief that when God speaks something more than an exchange of information takes place. When we hear God's voice stuff happens. We are changed. To hear God speak—and by hearing him become transformed—followers of Jesus don't delve into their own hearts or climb to the top of mountains to listen to the wind. Neither do we order bestsellers on Amazon, thinking they hold the key to communicating with God. When we want to hear God's voice, we go to God's Word. We turn to the scriptures. We open the Bible.

Talking Trees

That's not to say that God is utterly silent apart from the scriptures. If God is the maker of all that we see, then there will be evidence of his existence and insights into his will and ways all over the place. In the same way that a stroll through an exhibition of a particular artist's work will allow you to glean some truths about the woman who held the brush or sculpted the clay, life in this world yields innumerable insights about God. And as we seek to discern and appreciate them, we are hearing his voice, or least the faint echoes of it. The truths of human conscience bind most sane people together under a common morality; the beauty of a snowcapped mountain range that makes us all stop and stare, the complexity of life even at the cellular level, and the unfathomable expanse of the Universe all tell us *something*, don't they?

A few years ago, I was walking with my daughter through the Muir Woods National Monument outside San Francisco. The monument is made of more than 500 acres of old growth redwood trees. As we walked the trails, chins to the sky, we marveled at trees that were 800 years old and stood 200 feet tall. It was stunning. And on those trails, in that moment, I could hear what felt to me like the voice of God bouncing between pillars of red bark. Such beauty was no accident. Could a universe of meaningless chaos forge something as awe-inspiring as this grove? The trees, to me, were talking. I could hear God saying, "I am real."

God has a way of speaking through the realities, intricacies, and beauties of life and creation. But there's a limit to what is communicated. Take those redwood trees, for example. They tell me, and countless others who've strolled beneath them, *that* God exists. But what they can't tell me is precisely *who* this God is. Remember, it's not as though one can uproot a redwood, look at its roots, and find a tag that says, "Made by Jesus." That'd be helpful, but that's not how it works. The beauty of creation only offers us the most basic of divine revelation. Despite the many hints it offers and the abundant evidence it gives, God remains largely hidden. For specifics about God and to hear his voice with clarity and confidence, we must leave the woods and open his Word.

Starving in the Cereal Aisle

Despite Christianity's claim that God's voice can be heard in the pages of scripture—as well as in the preaching that proclaims its truths and the consolation of a friend who offers its promises—fewer and fewer people are actually reading it. And there are lots of reasons why. For some, it's a matter of not knowing where to begin. Do you just open it up to Genesis and work your way to the end? For others, it's a matter of being distracted. How can reading the Bible compete with binge-watching the latest hit series on Netflix or mindlessly scrolling on social media?

According to recent surveys, some ninety percent of homes, nearly every household in the United States, has a Bible. The most popular of Bible apps, published by YouVersion, has been installed more than five hundred million times on mobile devices. And yet, nearly thirty percent of Americans say that they've never read it. Even twenty percent of self-described "regular churchgoers" leave the Bible on the shelf or the app untapped, saying they rarely, if ever, read the Word. It should be no surprise then that fifty percent of high schoolers think that Sodom and Gomorrah were husband and wife, and sixty percent of Americans fail to name five of the Ten Commandments.[1]

Is it possible to starve to death in the aisle of a supermarket surrounded by shelves that are stocked full? Technically, yes. But it's only possible if said starving person is tragically ignorant, not knowing

---

[1] This is largely survey data compiled in a 2016 article by Albert Mohler decrying the growing problem of biblical illiteracy. The data seems to be derived from work done by Barna.org and research.lifeway.com. ("The Scandal of Biblical Illiteracy: It's Our Problem," albertmohler.com, January 20, 2016, https://albertmohler.com/2016/01/20 /the-scandal-of-biblical-illiteracy-its-our-problem-4.)

where they are, or self-destructively arrogant, thinking they're too good for the food right in front of them. This seems to be the situation for many if not most Americans when it comes to spirituality. We are dying to hear from God, while at the same time surrounded by and fully stocked with his Word. There's a Bible on every shelf and a corresponding app installed on every phone. We either don't know how close we are to hearing his voice, or we think we're too good to take a listen. Either way, we are starving.

But if we're willing to grab the Bible and crack it open or tap the app and take a listen, good things await us. The scriptures themselves are replete with the promise of insight, guidance, the gift of faith, and so much more straight from God. The psalmist writes, "The unfolding of your words gives light; it imparts understanding to the simple" (Psalm 119:130). Martin Luther had this to say about the power of the scriptures: "The Bible is alive, it speaks to me; it has feet, it runs after me; it has hands, it lays hold of me."[2] More than just ink on a page or verses spouted off by some preacher, the truth of the scriptures—the very voice of God—is like yeast in the flour. If we allow it to get into the mix of our lives, stuff starts to happen.

Some, on this point, push back. They argue, "Why should we have to open a book or sit under the preaching of its truths to

---

[2] These words, while attributed to Luther, cannot be sourced as quoted. The closest equivalent seems to be these words from Luther's famous Table Talks: "The words of our Savior Christ are exceeding powerful; *they have hands and feet*; they outdo the utmost subtleties of the worldly-wise..." (Martin Luther, *The Familiar Discourses of Dr. Martin Luther*, ed. Joseph Kerby, trans. Henry Bell [Oxford University, 1818].)

encounter God? Shouldn't it be easier and more accessible than that?" My rebuttal is simple: how much easier or more accessible could it possibly be? Other traditions, like Buddhism, have you meditating and sacrificing for years to *potentially* get in touch with the divine or achieve a state of nirvana. Others say that hearing God's voice with clarity and confidence is simply not possible, relegating you to a life of divine inklings and subjective experiences. So, yes, in the Christian faith, to hear from God, you'll need to read; you'll have to listen. It will take time. It requires a bit of effort. But that's how the world works. If you want to get fit, you have to go for a run or drive to the gym. If you want to learn about World War II you need to stream a documentary and download a few books. If you want to eat what Mom made for dinner then you have to saddle up to the table. And if you'd like to encounter God—to hear his voice and experience his power—you'll need to place yourself under his Word.

The True Purpose

For Christians, the point of reading the Bible isn't to know the Bible. The point is to know and encounter God. Sure, biblical knowledge is helpful; it's not a bad thing to have a head filled with facts from the scriptures. But if all you have is information after reading the Bible then you've missed out. The Bible wasn't given to us to communicate facts about God. Its purpose is to facilitate an encounter with God.

Jesus was surrounded by religious experts. As he preached and performed miracles, he was trailed and, at times, harassed by a group of spiritual leaders who knew the Torah inside and out.

And yet, despite their impressive knowledge these leaders failed to grasp just who Jesus was. Eventually, Jesus confronted them, saying,

> You search the scriptures because you think that in them you have eternal life; and it is they that bear witness about me, yet you refuse to come to me that you may have life. (John 5:39)

The spiritual leaders hounding Jesus believed that mere knowledge of God's Word was the key to eternal life. But if citing Bible verses alone could save them, then even the Devil would have a home in heaven.[3] Jesus made it plain to his adversaries: the point of reading the scriptures is to see that the scriptures point to him. But they refused. The purpose of reading God's Word is to encounter God himself. Specifically, the goal is to draw you toward faith in Jesus Christ, to show you who he is, to mesmerize you with the depth of God's love on display in the work that he's done, and to set your feet firmly in the promises that are true for you because of his life, death, and resurrection. That's it. That's why we read the scriptures.

And yet, as we approach the scriptures, it's all too easy to fall in line with Jesus's adversaries. You might not fancy yourself a religious leader, but like them we easily open God's Word with the wrong purpose in mind. Some people study the scriptures to feel smart and

---

[3] At the start of Jesus's earthly ministry, he spent forty days fasting in the wilderness. (See Matthew 4:1-11) At the height of his hunger the Devil appeared, tempting Jesus. The Devil demonstrates a knowledge of scripture, which he twists in his attempt to lure Jesus out of his task of being faithful in the face of temptation on humanity's behalf. Jesus displays his own (far superior) knowledge of scripture, citing it forcefully and correctly in response to the Devil's attempts.

superior in a world where knowledge is power. There are those who familiarize themselves with its stories and truths for the sole purpose of manipulating and controlling others. And still some scour its pages, thinking it's a science textbook or an encyclopedia filled with facts on every facet of life. But if we come to the scriptures with any such agenda we are no different than the religious leaders who hovered around Jesus. We're missing the point. We open the Bible to encounter the divine, but the divine is not the knowledge, power, or data that we derive from its pages. The divine encounter is with Jesus. It all bears witness about him and it draws us to lean upon him, to place our hope in him, and to find life in him.

Searching for Jesus

Not long ago, my family and I were on vacation in Colorado, hiking the trails of Rocky Mountain National Park. Our favorite part of the trip was venturing into the park near dusk when the animals who called it home would come out to graze. My six-year-old son, Jack, could not contain his excitement as he scanned the horizon, searching for moose, elk, and our favorite, bighorn sheep. Every few minutes, he would whisper a reminder to the entire family: "Psst, guys! Be sure to *peel your eyes!*" I didn't have the heart to correct him. He was close enough. And besides, his version—while somehow gross compared to "keep your eyes peeled"—was cute. And effective. With peeled eyes, we stayed on task, searching for sheep.

The point of reading the scriptures is to encounter Jesus. And since, as author Sally Lloyd-Jones puts it, "Every word whispers his name," we approach it with our hearts and minds on high alert. With eyes peeled we fix our attention on the horizon of each word and phrase, seeking to catch a glimpse of how it points us to Christ.

Jesus himself approached the scriptures this way. Early in Jesus's earthly ministry, he visited his hometown synagogue on the Sabbath. Handed the scroll of Isaiah, he stood up, as was the custom, to offer a reading:

> Jesus unrolled the scroll and found the place where it was written, "The Spirit of the Lord is upon me, because he has anointed me to proclaim good news to the poor. He has sent me to proclaim liberty to the captives and recovering of sight to the blind, to set at liberty those who are oppressed, to proclaim the year of the Lord's favor." And he rolled up the scroll and gave it back to the attendant and sat down. And the eyes of all in the synagogue were fixed on him. And he began to say to them, "Today this scripture has been fulfilled in your hearing." (Luke 4:17-21)

Jesus couldn't have been any clearer. Jesus believed himself to be the fulfillment of Isaiah's words. He was the one sent to proclaim good news to the poor. He was the one through whom freedom and healing would come. He was the one who would usher in the favor of God. Though they were given some 700 years before he was born, Jesus read the words of Isaiah as though he was looking in a mirror and seeing his own image.

The scriptures as a whole, from Genesis to Revelation, tell a single story. It's a story of creation, corruption, salvation, and restoration. It starts in a garden, where humankind ushers in sin and divorces itself from communion with the Divine. And it ends with the promise of an eternal city in a re-created and perfected reality, where God's people are gathered and his presence is so close—so bright—that there is no need for the sun. And Jesus is at the center of it all. Not just chronologically; his presence, his promises, and the work he accomplished in his life, death, and resurrection—and someday in his return—are like threads that run through each part and passage.

To put it simply, everything in the Old Testament, all thirty-nine books, points *toward* Jesus. They predict him, promise him, and foreshadow him. A case can be made that every major character we encounter in the Old Testament offers us a glimpse, in their own way, of Christ and what he would accomplish in his death and resurrection. For example, Adam was unfaithful to God in the Garden of Eden, ushering sin into the world. But Jesus is faithful to the very end, bringing salvation. Moses led God's people, the Israelites, out of captivity to Egypt. Jesus leads humanity out of captivity to sin and death. David, though small in stature and armed only with rocks, slays the giant, Goliath. Jesus, in weakness, destroys the monster that is death when he rolls back the stone on Easter morning. The list goes on and on. Jesus is the truer and better version of every character and subplot we see in the Old Testament.

Likewise, everything in the New Testament, all twenty-seven books, flows *from* Jesus. The gospels capture his teachings and tell the story of his life. The rest—an inspired compilation of letters passed among the earliest churches, Christians, and pastors—expound on what we know to be true about God in light of Jesus and proclaim the incredible implications of his work.

The Old Testament points *toward Jesus*. The New Testament flows *from Jesus*. He binds it together and without him it falls apart. Without him it makes no sense. Without him the story told in the pages of the Bible would not be worth telling, let alone believing. Because without him this story has no heart, no soul, no hope.

God has a lot to say. And spoiler alert: it's really good news. To hear it we turn to the truths of God's Word and discover that every passage is ushering us toward something specific, and it's not a list of rules to memorize or a religious system to master. No, it's moving us toward a person. To hear God's voice we lay hold of the scriptures and we tune our senses to find Jesus. We ask ourselves, "How is this pointing me to Christ?"

Do Versus Done

There is a distinction at work in God's Word that is essential to grasp. Failure to do so can lead to all kinds of confusion when trying to hear God's voice and rob you of the encouragement and comfort meant to come from the scriptures. It's the difference between two very simple words: "do" and "done."

The Bible is filled with commands from God for his people. These commands show us how to live as members of his family and guide us in what it looks like to thrive in our calling as humans. When you read the Bible or listen to teaching derived from it you'll hear any number of things that we should *do*. The shorthand for these expectations is referred to by Christians as the law. The other aspect of God's Word is the gospel or the good news. The gospel has a much narrower definition; it's the declaration of what Jesus Christ has accomplished for the world. Specifically, it's the message of what he's done for you.

And what has he done for you? In his perfect life, he's satisfied every expectation laid upon you. With his death on the cross he's earned forgiveness for every sin. And with his rise out of the grave he's set you free from the punishment and condemnation that comes with failing to keep God's law. In short, the gospel is the message that everything is *done* for you in Jesus Christ. Or, to use Jesus's own words, "It is finished."[4]

This distinction in God's Word is important for understanding the dynamic at work in us as we encounter it. And here's where things get really interesting. We flip open a bible or settle in for the sermon at church hoping to hear from God. But God has an agenda of his own that he's looking to accomplish too. And it all takes place in and through the law and the gospel, through the "do" and the "done." As you're confronted with something that strikes you as a command or an expectation the goal that God has is for those words to convict you, to reveal the need for you to accomplish that thing but—most importantly—to show that you haven't. The aim of the law is to force you to confront and confess your failures. And in doing so, to create a need, a hunger, and an appreciation for Christ and all that he's accomplished. The aim of the law is to lead you to lean upon the gospel. Scripture shows you what you've failed to do for God so that you might leap for joy at what God, in Christ, has done for you.

---

[4] "When Jesus had received the sour wine, he said, 'It is finished,' and he bowed his head and gave up his spirit." (John 19:30) These last words of Jesus summarize the entirety of Jesus's message and the work of his ministry. He has done everything to make all things right between humanity and our Creator. Nothing needs to be added to or detracted from it. It (the whole work of salvation) is finished in his suffering and death.

For example, look at what Jesus says in his most famous teaching and then let's compare it to some of his last words as he's being crucified. In Matthew 5 Jesus is sitting on a mountainside with a crowd gathered, and he begins to teach them about the kingdom of God. Among the many things he says, he offers this:

I say to you, love your enemies and pray for those who persecute you so that you may be sons of your Father who is in heaven. (Matthew 5:44-45)

In these words Jesus is communicating the standard of what's expected of God's people in God's kingdom. We are to love and forgive like no other, even our enemies. This is clearly a command. It's a "do" if there ever was one.

And yet, if you really sit with it, if you honestly wrestle with it, you'll have to confess just how awful you are at living this out. And you're not alone. Every one of us, at an instinctual level, is revolted by the notion of showing such kindness and grace to those who've hurt us. Sitting with this command from Jesus we are forced to confront how we utterly fail to comply with this command. We can't do it—not completely, not joyfully, not wholeheartedly.

But then jump to Jesus's words in Luke 23:

[W]hen they came to the place that is called The Skull, there they crucified him, and the criminals, one on his right and one on his left. And Jesus said, "Father, forgive them, for they know not what they do." (Luke 23:33-34)

Jesus is being murdered by his enemies. They've falsely accused him, his friends have betrayed and denied him, the Roman authorities have been convinced to crucify him, and his persecutors are high-fiving as he bleeds, slowly suffocates, and ultimately dies. But in the midst of it all, at the high point of the hurt and pain for Jesus, what do we see him doing? What does he say? He intercedes for their forgiveness. He puts the best possible construction on their actions ("they don't know what they are doing") and asks for God the Father to show them grace, to give them mercy. Jesus is living out the very command he gave to us. What we can't do, what we refuse to do, Jesus is willingly and perfectly accomplishing. In that moment on the cross Jesus is dying for us. He is serving as the just sacrifice for all of our atrocities. But he is also keeping the law for us. He is living it completely until the very end.

In the scriptures, as we come across the commands, the things we must do, they are meant to inform and shape and guide our lives. More than anything, they are meant to show us who we are, or more specifically, who we are *not*. They exist to create a hunger for the work of Jesus. God's commands in the scripture create a need for God's son, who is the focus and the fulfillment of the scriptures.

To hear God's voice we open the scriptures and grapple with the things God says we should do, we apply them to our lives and wrestle deeply with what they reveal to us about ourselves. We then ask these important questions: "Has the cross of Christ forgiven the failures they reveal? And does the faithfulness of Christ cover over the disobedience that I discover?" The answer to both is ever and always yes. And it's what God wants you to hear each and every day.

Plans are Good

Most people don't read the Bible because they have no idea how to begin. It's a big book. And for many, just opening up to Genesis and diving in doesn't work. The best way to begin reading the scriptures and to hear what God has to say is to work from a plan. Here's one that I suggest and that may very well work for you:

1. Live in the gospels
2. Pray the Psalms
3. Study the rest

The Christian faith teaches that "all of scripture is breathed out by God and profitable," as Paul says to Timothy. Meaning that it's all worth your time. But if you do anything, soak up Matthew, Mark, Luke, and John. And in doing so, become best friends with the life, teaching, death, and resurrection of Jesus. Since the entirety of scripture flows to him and from him you might as well spend the bulk of your time with him.

Then, use the Psalms to pray. The Psalms were the prayer book of God's people long before the arrival of Jesus. They give voice to every emotion and every need that humans have as we live in this fallen world. There's nothing you can go through in life that the Psalms can't relate to and give you words to help express. Plus, they provide another means of drawing close to Jesus. Many of the Psalms point to him and the promises he fulfills, and the entire book itself was known to Jesus and prayed through by Jesus during his life and ministry. By praying the Psalms you are not just praying words that point to Christ but that Jesus himself has uttered countless times before.

Lastly, work through the rest of scripture in sincere study. Granted, that's a lot, but don't feel pressure to become some kind of biblical scholar or the person who knows all the obscure answers in a game of Bible trivia. Besides, is anyone actually playing Bible trivia, and if so, do you really want to be at that party? But do take a deep dive into Paul's letter to the Romans and contemplate what it means to be right with God "apart from the law." You should walk through the Book of Job and ponder the question of trusting in God in the face of unmerited suffering. And it's never been easier to be a casual student of the rest of the Bible. Podcasts and apps abound, as do devotional books and commentaries on the scriptures.[5] Each of these helps make the scriptures more accessible, understandable, and relatable for those simply trying to invite the voice of God into their everyday lives.

Not Alone

Despite all of this, you may have no interest in opening the Bible. If so, you're not alone. Most people will never crack open the scriptures or listen to a sermon preached from its pages. Even among those who claim to have a very high view of the Bible, when pressed about how much they actually engage with it, the majority admit that it's far less often than they'd like.[6]

---

[5] The publisher of this book (1517.org) offers some of the best, most Christ-centered resources in the world for those seeking to grasp the message of Jesus and the whole story of the scriptures. For example, I cannot suggest enough *The Christ Key: Unlocking the Centrality of Christ in the Old Testament* by Chad Bird.

[6] "State of the Bible 2021: Five Key Findings," Barna Group, May 19, 2021, https://www.barna.com/research/sotb-2021/.

But let's return to those headphones, shall we? They represent the idea one can hear from God; we can listen to the voice of the Divine. And the truth is we are all plugged into something; we're all connected to some kind of source, searching for inspiration, comfort, encouragement, and direction. We're all listening for the gifts and the goods that, if we are honest, only God can give in any satisfying sense. The question is, what are you listening to and can it deliver?

Which brings us back to the Bible that we don't read. Even if you don't think it's inspired, you need to ask yourself this: in a world where everyone is listening for God and searching for his voice, how and why have the scriptures endured?

The French writer and enlightenment philosopher François-Marie Arouet, better known by his nom de plume Voltaire, sought with passion to rid his country of Christian influence during the French Revolution. Voltaire is quoted as saying, "It is impossible that Christianism survives."[7] He's also credited with declaring that, within a hundred years, no one would know of the Bible except as an artifact in museums. While likely apocryphal, the sentiment fits with the philosopher's well-documented attitude toward the scriptures. Needless to say, Voltaire was wrong. So wrong, in fact, that when his home was auctioned after his death, it was purchased by the French Bible Society. Despite people disregarding it, critics attacking it, tyrants trying to eliminate it, and skeptics dismissing it, the Word of God just keeps going.

Why is that? Why does it endure? Maybe it's just because people love old books and ancient stories. Maybe. Or perhaps it's because

---

[7] Eugène Noël, *Voltaire*, (Paris, F. Chamerot, 1855).

there's something more to be found within its pages? What if the reason it has endured—despite detractors and disinterest—is because it is the very voice of the Divine? What if it's the thing you need to plug into in order to receive the things you know you need and can only get, in any satisfying way, from God himself? What if?

Do you want to encounter God? Do you want to hear the voice of the one who made you and learn of his love for you, his plans for you, and of the larger story he's invited you into?

Take a second and think. Do you?

Me too.

Are you feeling far from him? Are you wondering where you stand or what it means to follow him? Open the Word—sit with it, draw near to it, listen to it—and you'll find him.

But be ready; you'll be hearing one name over and over. It's the name of the One whom the scriptures intend to drive you toward, the One every story points to and every truth flows from. The One who's done what you won't and accomplished what you can't. The One who has lived, died, and risen for you.

Be ready, because when the Word speaks it shouts "Jesus."

Taking Inventory

Perhaps it comes as no surprise that the goal of God's relating to us is to point us, time and again, to the person and work of Christ. But that's not all he's up to. This personal God also has a plan for your life; he has a road set apart for you to walk. But discerning that plan and walking that road is yet another place where spirituality easily gets off track.

Chances are you've felt the pull, in one direction or the other, of what we will discuss in the next chapter. It's time for us to talk about the tendency to frame spirituality as a life obsessed with rules, either keeping them in pursuit of purity or breaking them in the name of freedom.

QUESTIONS TO CONSIDER:

Do you believe that you've heard God speak to you? If not, why do you think that is? If so, what was it like? How was it communicated to you (a feeling, a voice) and what did he say?

How would you describe your relationship with the Bible? Are you familiar and comfortable with it, or does the idea of reading it seem intimidating or perhaps a bit pointless? What gets in the way of you experiencing the Christian scriptures more frequently than you do now?

How do you feel knowing that the primary purpose of the Bible is to point you to Christ? If the Bible has but one focus, Jesus, how is it worthwhile to continually read and study it?

SIX

On Pietists and Party Animals

"And now that you don't have to be perfect, you can be good."

—JOHN STEINBECK, *EAST OF EDEN*

NOBODY LIKES A CHEATER. But everybody likes catching one. Maybe that's why so many people love to hate on Tom Brady, the winningest quarterback in NFL history. He stands alone, having played in eleven Super Bowl games and taken home seven Super Bowl rings as champion. He was crowned the league's most valuable player three times and won Super Bowl MVP a record five times. Not only that, but the final championship he won was at the age of forty-three. The average NFL star plays just over three seasons in the league before retiring. Tom Brady won the Super Bowl in his twenty-first.

Such unparalleled success is bound to breed its skeptics, people certain that Brady must have gamed the system to gain an unfair advantage. Is he under-inflating footballs for a better grip in cold weather? Perhaps his team is secretly filming the practice sessions of upcoming opponents? What if he's taking performance-enhancing drugs or undergoing some kind of radical gene therapy to keep him at the top of his game? Maybe being married to a supermodel filled him with an unmatched (and frankly unfair!) level of confidence on the field? These are all questions that have been asked. And yet, despite the desire of so many to catch Brady in some kind of underhanded activity that can explain away his success, he was never caught red-handed. He will go down in history, to the frustration of many, as simply a winner.[1]

But don't expect the conspiracy theories to go away or those who question his success to quiet down; it's just too much fun. Whether it's in the sports we watch, the work we do, or the friends and neighbors we live alongside and compare ourselves to, when we see success, we are tempted to assume it's a scam. We can't help but wonder which corners were cut or which rules were bent.

But we would be wise to ask, where does it come from? Why is it that we love catching cheaters and calling fouls? The assumption of many is that it has divine origins. We learned it from God.

The Whistle

Buried in your junk drawer is a whistle, the old-school kind made of brass and attached to a long, white cotton lanyard. It's the kind of whistle your elementary gym teacher always had hanging from her neck, even when she wasn't in class. It's likely left over from when you served as a referee in your nephew's soccer league or

---

[1] Even after his retirement in 2023 and the end of his once storybook, supermodel marriage the debate around Tom Brady and his legacy is sure to continue, likely for decades. We just can't seem to get our fill of poking holes in perfection and assessing someone else's performance.

that time you volunteered as a crossing guard at the local elementary school.

Lifting it from the drawer, you pause and untangle the thing from a mess of other items that have decided to hitch a ride, wrapping themselves in the sweat-stained rope of the whistle. Once it's free, you can't help yourself. You give it a chirp. Sure enough, despite its age, it sounds great. More than that, it *feels* great. Who doesn't love blowing a whistle? Calling a foul, stopping play when someone steps out of bounds, having the ability to grab everyone's attention when things aren't as they should be, is a power trip that few can resist.

The whistle represents the fact that for many, if not most, religion is about learning to play within a certain set of rules. Faith is a game of grasping what's right and what's wrong, discerning what activities are allowed, and then avoiding anything that God has labeled as "out of bounds." In such a spirituality, success equals playing God's game as best you can lest he—the Big Referee in the sky—tosses you from his field. The whistle doesn't hang from our necks but his. There's a belief that God loves to call fouls and catch cheaters *more* than we do. He strolls the sidelines of our lives, watching and waiting for us to do something stupid or to catch us red-handed trying to game his system. So, play right and follow his rules. If you do so, you might just win the game, get a Gatorade bath of grace, and head to heaven—or Disneyworld—to celebrate.

Sound at all familiar? I thought so.

The problems presented to us by the whistle are many, and we'll tackle the biggest in the pages ahead. But let's start with the very notion of God and his rules. Certainly, God has a standard for his creation. But the issue one immediately runs into with the idea of a whistle is that the boundary lines of right religion seem so blurry, so confusing and contradictory.

Depending on which church you go to or believer you talk to, God's rules seem to shift and change. Some churches claim that God only blows the whistle on big things, like murder. "Don't kill anybody, and you'll be cool." Other churches hear the whistle being blown over everything. "Don't drink. Don't dance. Don't vote for Democrats." And then there are some churches that say the whistle actually never gets blown at all. The only sin in those churches is believing that there's such a thing as sin in the first place. So, which is it? Where are the lines? What *are* the expectations?

Great questions. Let's start there.

In The Beginning

In Genesis chapter 1 we hear the story of God creating all things. But not only do we see God making all things, we get a sense of God's intention for all things:

> So God created man in his own image, in the image of God he created him; male and female he created them. And God blessed them. And God said to them, "Be fruitful and multiply and fill the earth and subdue it and have dominion over the fish of the sea and over the birds of the heavens and over every living thing that moves on the earth." (Genesis 1:27-28)

God made all that exists and then handed it to humanity. And in handing it to us, he tasked us with the job of taking the incredible raw material that is this world and making something more with it. Specifically, our job is to imitate him. Just as he made something out of nothing for us to enjoy, we are to take the something that he made and be makers ourselves, harnessing the potential of creation in a way that builds on its beauty, draws out its potential, and leads to its (and our!) flourishing. That's what it means to "have dominion."

And why would God bless[2] us with this task? Because when we live it out, it brings glory to his name and adds joy to our lives. When we tease out even greater beauty and blessing from this incredible reality that he's placed us in by building families, creating culture, and making discoveries, it only adds to the glory that's due his name. After all, it's his design. It was all his idea. And the work of being a maker, a creator, of imitating our God is incredibly satisfying. It makes our lives richer and fuller, infusing them with purpose and delight.

It's hard to overstate the implications of this point. God does not want us to run scared from life in this world. He didn't create us to live with a fearful hesitation, afraid to do something wrong. His intention was for us to confidently and freely enjoy life in this world. We are to hold tight to that mandate to be makers, cultivators, and enjoyers of this world. If we hold back in fear of failure or of God calling foul, we miss out. The call to create and enjoy is what drives us toward forging life-changing relationships, making incredible music, discovering breakthrough medicines, and to create far too many *The Fast & Furious* movies.

God did not place us in this world just so he could police us as we tiptoe around the Garden of Eden, afraid to make a false move. He made us to unleash us and to enjoy us, as he watched us dive into the world that he'd given to us

---

[2] Genesis 1:28 is often referred to as the creation mandate or the culture mandate. This verse starts with an important and often overlooked truth, that the call to create and to be fruitful is a blessing. It's not a curse to work, to create and to labor in love and service to the world around us. The curse would come later, in Genesis 3. But it doesn't erase God's intention, design, and desire for our work. It's an invitation to enjoy something that he himself delights in, being a creator and a caretaker.

Corruption

That was ideal. But you know what happened next—Genesis chapter 3. I'll give you a summary: we screwed it all up. Adam and Eve, our spiritual ancestors, rebelled against God's authority. Discontent[3] with being made in God's image, they bought the lie that God was holding them back from something greater, being gods themselves. To say the absolute least, the effects of this rebellion were enormous. It led to humanity being disconnected from God's family and condemned to pay for its sins in the form of death. It also flooded the human heart, and every atom of creation, with all kinds of dysfunction.

It started out so good, so perfect. But after Genesis 3, it was all broken. The whole thing had been corrupted.

A major effect of the Fall was that it not only destroyed our relationship with God, but it spoiled our relationship with creation. We no longer instinctively lay hold of this world and live out the mandate

---

[3] Martin Luther noted that all sin has its root in this original discontent. All that's bad and broken in us flows from our desire to be our own God and to find a way to be complete (to be right or just) apart from him. As such, all sin is really a breaking of the first commandment: "You shall not have any other gods before me." (Exodus 20:3) This is discussed in greater detail in chapter eight.

Luther had this to say: All those who do not at all times trust God and do not in all their works or sufferings, life and death, trust in His favor, grace and goodwill, but seek His favor in other things or in themselves, do not keep this [First] Commandment, and practice real idolatry, even if they were to do the works of all the other Commandments, and in addition had all the prayers, obedience, patience, and chastity of all the saints combined. For the chief work is not present, without which all the others are nothing but mere sham, show and pretense, with nothing back of them… If we doubt or do not believe that God is gracious to us and is pleased with us, or if we presumptuously expect to please Him only through and after our works, then it is all pure deception, outwardly honoring God, but inwardly setting up self as a false [savior].... (Martin Luther, *Treatise Concerning Good Works*, 1520; Part X. XI).

of Genesis 1 in a way that increases our joy and draws us closer to God. We now allow the things that we create and the stuff that we use to control us and diminish our flourishing. Devoid of a life-giving relationship with our Creator, we look at the stuff of this world and give it dominion over *us*, affording it influence and seeking peace from it that should only be given to and sought from God himself. Rather than subdue creation, we make an idol out of it, and it very often, so very easily, subdues us.

A glass of wine goes from an occasional enjoyment to a constant companion and a chemical dependence, a coping mechanism for avoiding feelings of stress or shame or anything uncomfortable. A new phone or a better television goes from something you save up for to something you need so badly that you'll pile debt upon debt to have it. Reality television or professional sports go from an amusement you enjoy to something you spend so much time watching and discussing that one could argue you're more interested in staring at the lives of others than in living your own.

Let's reflect for a minute: where do you see the stuff of this world controlling you and consuming you?

In my own life, it comes down to two things: social media and my work as a pastor. I don't just post and scroll on social media. If I'm being honest, I use each post and every scroll to indulge a desire I have to compare myself to others and as a means of fueling an incessant thirst I have for affirmation. *That's* why I open the apps dozens of times each day. "My perfectly timed tweet about the latest cultural flashpoint got more likes and retweets than my colleague! I'm witty and lovable, and my voice matters!"

My work as a pastor plays a critical role in upholding my sense of worth and meaning. When I'm logging long hours, I convince myself that it's proof of my goodness as a person, and when I'm feeling needed by parishioners and indispensable to my staff members, I convince myself that I'm truly important. And I use it all to legitimize my being lazy or lax in other responsibilities, like home and family and tending to my own physical and spiritual well-being. "It's okay to be late for dinner or to forsake a bit of exercise; I'm a good guy doing indispensable work!"

What about you? Is it shopping online and a growing pile of credit card debt? Is it your own health and fitness? Our bodies were given as gifts to enjoy and blessings to care for, but we can easily turn "wellness" into something we worship. Or perhaps it's politics. Good government is a product of humankind thriving under the mandate to cultivate and care for this world. But the push and pull for power within that system can quickly hijack our hopes and fears and consume our lives. For many, it's a battle with lust. Attractiveness and sexuality are incredible gifts that God has baked into our existence. But appreciation of these gifts can quickly turn into looks that linger and minds that race whenever we encounter an attractive neighbor.

Whatever it is for you and however it manifests itself for you, it's the same struggle for you as it is for me and every member of the human race. It's our backward and broken relationship with creation rearing its ugly head. What was supposed to be subdued by us now has control over us. But we are not victims; the bondage is self-inflicted. First by Adam and Eve and every day after by you and me.

Rather than worship God and enjoy his world, we worship the world and drive ourselves away from God.

This is what Christians are talking about when we talk about sin. It's taking the good things of this world, using them and abusing them in such a way that we do harm to ourselves and our neighbors, showing ourselves to be far from the God who made us and from the way of life that he intended for us. And God does, in fact, "blow the whistle" over such sin. He calls it out in his Word and convicts us of it by the power of his Holy Spirit. He confronts us with the reality of our dysfunction and awakens us to the truth of how messed up things are.

But he doesn't leave us in despair. No, he meets us in that place of anguish over sin, and he preaches the gospel to us. He proclaims the message of forgiveness for all sin and of reconciliation with him, the Father, that is ours through the work of Jesus Christ, his son. And then—having breathed life into us—he invites us to step into a new relationship and a fresh dynamic with both him and creation. He invites us, each day, to live and move, knowing that his love and favor are present realities and current possessions. And to see the whole of creation—every aspect of life in this world—as something to humbly subdue and a gift to enjoy according to his design, rather than something to obsess over and idolize to our demise. He invites us to grow in the knowledge that he loves us fully and to discern each day what it means to love and enjoy this world rightly.

Let's Get Legal

There is general agreement in the wide world of the Christian faith that humankind's dysfunctional relationship with God and his creation is a fact. Where people of faith begin to part ways, in rather drastic style, has to do with the way in which we respond to this fact. In general, the temptation is to respond by heading, at full sprint, toward one of two extremes: legalism or license. Let's start with legalism.

The thinking goes like this: "Since there's a risk of us misusing, abusing, or outright idolizing certain things in God's world, then let's just stay far away from those things." In a really simplistic sense, the logic works. If you don't drink, then you can't get drunk. If you don't go to the club and dance with tipsy and other mutually "thirsty" young adults, you're less likely to hook up. If you don't own a television, a laptop, a phone, a tablet, or any other streaming-capable kind of device, then you'll never get caught up in binge-watching eight seasons of a highly questionable but deeply entertaining HBO drama, becoming so obsessed that you lie, calling into work "sick" just so you can stay in bed all day and see how it ends. Problem solved, right?

Those who run toward legalism lean hard on the idea that God is an overactive referee, wanting to blow the whistle like crazy. And in an effort to please him or to avoid being called out by him, the legalist, in essence, takes the whistle off of God's neck and places it around their own. The legalist believes that they can beat God at his own sin-spotting game, getting a few steps ahead by calling their own fouls *first*, putting rules in place to prevent the truly egregious abuses from happening in the first place. The byproduct, among other things, are communities of faith with a hyper focus on piety[4], on lives

---

[4] Pietism as a religious reform movement began in the seventeenth-century among German Lutherans. Its focus on personal faith and the lived experience of the believer as a primary source of assurance and comfort in the faith parted ways with traditional Lutheran theological emphases. The piety movement likely laid the

marked by a vigorous and visible commitment to what gets defined in their circles as simply "holy living."

While well intended, legalism or hyper-pietism is ultimately an over-correction, careening from one ditch directly into another. By placing the whistle on their own necks and adding rules on top of rules, legalists step into the errors of minimizing their sins and demonizing God's good creation.

I used to play a lot of golf. I say "used to play" because the game of golf requires two things that, since entering the ministry and starting a family, I have very little of: time and money. But back in the day when I used to play, I noticed something interesting about golfers. When we would hit a bad shot, we tended not to blame ourselves, our swing, our stance, or our grip—at least, not right away. Our instinct was to blame the club. "Yep. I told you I need a new driver!" This instinct baffled me, though I myself was guilty of indulging it. If it was really about the quality of the club, then how did guys shoot fifteen under par, back in 1918, with the equivalent of a rock tied to a tree limb? But I suppose blaming the equipment is easier to say to the rest of your foursome than the more accurate statement of, "I'm

---

foundation for American evangelical Christianity, which places an intense focus on the personal conversion experience as well as providing proof of genuine faith through moral living. It has also, in this author's opinion, contributed to a hyper-individualization of spirituality that we now see and which has been noted earlier in this book. All of this serves to rob people of the comfort and peace that the message of Jesus is meant to provide. The original Lutherans had it right. When we want to know if, how, and why we are "saved," we should not look at ourselves. Doing so will only give us more opportunity to doubt God's love or to be distracted from God's love. Instead, we look to the word of Christ—who he is and what he's done for us—and to the sacraments of baptism and the Lord's Supper where we can see God at work, objectively, saving and sustaining sinners.

clearly not good at this game." Truth is, it's not the club; it's the person holding it. Legalism is like the guys on the golf course dissing their drivers and complaining about their putters. Legalism deals with sin by blaming the object. But the problem isn't the alcohol, the music, the latest show on Netflix, or the way the opposite sex decides to dress. The problem is you.

In Galatians chapter 2, the apostle Paul rails against the legalistic, pietistic impulse we all have, writing this:

> ...we know that a person is not justified by works of the law but through faith in Jesus Christ, so we also have believed in Christ Jesus, in order to be justified by faith in Christ and not by works of the law, because by works of the law no one will be justified. (Galatians 2:16)

Paul's words are important. Yes, we should be deadly serious about sin, and we should seek to honor God in all that we do. But that being said, there is nothing that one can do to keep themselves free from sin. There is no one so capable of keeping the law, of abiding by the rules, that the whistle would never need to be blown. No one could be so holy, so pious, as to make God say, "Wow! Look at how *good* she is! The way she keeps the rules makes it clear that she's got holiness figured out." It's not possible, and to expect or imply that one can please God is to seriously underestimate the depth of one's own dysfunction. And *that's* the secret irony of the legalist. It looks like he or she is more serious about sin than anyone else. But by demanding a certain level of holiness and demonizing creation, it betrays a lack of seriousness about their own sin. They fail to see just what the real problem is and how deep it runs. You could go full Amish, swearing off the internet, electronics, and automobiles. You could wear wool pants in the summer and build barns for fun. But here's the truth: you will still be a sinner. There is nothing one can do to make themselves or keep themselves holy. To live in fear of created things and pile up rules to avoid sin and prove one's devotion to the divine is nothing less than a rejection of the gospel itself. It says that the blame is not really with us but with the stuff around us, denying our need for salvation. It places the primary emphasis on curating a holy environment and writing God-pleasing maxims to live by, shifting the focus away from Christ and his forgiving work onto our own efforts.

Time to Party

The opposite of legalism is license, a complete disregard for anything resembling a holy life. Rather than blow the whistle every five minutes, the licentious person becomes a hedonist or a party animal and throws it away altogether. The thinking goes something like this: "Look, no one is perfect. So, what's the point in trying? Besides, you only live once. After all, God will forgive us." And they're off to Vegas.

Like the pietist, the licentious party animal is guilty of minimizing their sinfulness, downplaying the impact it has on their lives and on the people around them. They act as if their self-indulgence happens in a vacuum, affecting no one and nothing—not their friends and family, not their health and well-being, and certainly not their relationship with God. And like the pietist, the party animal has a dysfunctional relationship with creation. Whereas the pietist demonizes and blames created things for his struggles, the party animal idolizes creation. He places a premium on personal experience, prioritizing his existence around squeezing the greatest possible pleasure out of life.

Have you ever met someone who loves to tell others about how much their faith means to them and how committed they are to Jesus, yet, when you look at their life—the things they actually do—it screams the opposite message?[5] Their priorities seem seriously confused and their choices questionable for someone who claims to be a Christian. The whistle should be sounding off over more than a few things. But if it is, they either don't hear it, or they just don't care. That's a sign that there's likely an attitude of license—a party animal perspective—at work.

From my own struggles with this attitude, I can tell you that at the heart of it all is a *lie*. It's a lie they've begun to believe that enables their behavior. It's a lie that every follower of Jesus is susceptible to believing. It's a lie that goes something like this: "Because Jesus *loves* me, Jesus *lets* me," which, of course, is some seriously faulty logic. That'd be like my teenage daughter saying, "My dad loves me a lot. Which means when I get to college, I can forget my classes, set aside all morals, and just go *crazy*." That's not how it's supposed to work. One of the many reasons her mother and I have tried to love our daughter well is so that she won't have a boatload of parent-induced trauma to compensate for once she leaves the care of our home. Instead, firmly grasping the fact that she's loved by her family, she'll

---

[5] In fairness, this is all of us to some degree. We are all guilty of failing to love God as we ought. The claim of hypocrisy rings true for us all. As John puts it, saying we have no sin is the height of self-deception. (1 John 1:8)

resist the impulse to look for validation through wild self-indulgence. At least, that's the hope.

Take a look at how Paul responds to the lie that fuels the party animal perspective:

> But if, in our endeavor to be justified in Christ, we too were found to be sinners, is Christ then a servant of sin? Certainly not! (Galatians 2:17)

When forgiven people find a way to act like self-serving, wild, and crazy sinners, is it Jesus's fault? No. The grace that flows from his cross in no way enables or gives way to idolatry. Christ is no servant of sin. And those who continue to make him one, who insist on the lie that the love of Jesus gives license to all kinds of indulgence, they, too, are rejecting the gospel. They're rejecting it not because they are trying to earn their salvation—that's the legalist. They are rejecting the gospel by failing to value their salvation.

Our love of created things and our obsession with self is so evil, so corrosive to everything it touches, that in order for us to be rescued from its impact, God had to send his own son to be crushed and killed by it. He did this so that we could see where license ultimately leads: the harm of others—of even God himself—who try to call us out of ourselves and toward a life of love. He did it so that justice could be done, but in a way that would allow us to be spared. Christ was killed in our place, as though he was the God-rejecting, creation-abusing, relationship-destroying, self-obsessed party animal because that's what such behavior deserves. But in taking our place, Christ set us free.

If we grasp this, if we have any value or appreciation of this, how could we possibly continue to insist on serving our gut, buying the lie, and living only for ourselves? We can't. Each time we are confronted by the depth of our sin and the incredible sacrifice of Christ, we have no option but to say, "Thank you, Father, for this gift!" And then to ask a new question: "If I'm this *loved*, how then should I *live?*"

Liberty and Love

If a life of faith is not about legalism or license, then what is the goal? If it's not about avoiding sin by obsessing over the rules or indulging it and throwing them out altogether, then what's left? Two things, actually: liberty and love.

The life of faith is a life of freedom. We are set loose to ask a new set of questions, questions focused on the love of God and of others. And then following those answers wherever they lead. We can set questions like, "How do I get things *right* in life," or "How do I get the *most* out of life" aside. In Christ, those questions have been answered. We are right in the eyes of God and will enjoy life to the full through faith in Jesus.[6] We are now set free to focus on love. Take a look at how Paul puts it in Galatians 5:

> For you were called to freedom, brothers. Only do not use your freedom as an opportunity for the flesh, but through love serve one another. For the whole law is fulfilled in one word: "You shall love your neighbor as yourself." (Galatians 5:13-14)

Living in this freedom, we find ourselves asking questions like these: "Which choice properly expresses the love I have for God and the mercy he's shown me?" And, "Which choice will lead to the most

---

[6] "The thief comes only to steal and kill and destroy. I came that they may have life and have it abundantly." (John 10:10)

amount of love being felt by my coworker, my spouse, my irritable next-door neighbor, or my argumentative and ideologically opposite son-in-law?" Just imagine how differently your day might go, your life might feel, if those kinds of questions led the way.

Again, the way we get to this place of freedom—and remain anchored in it—is through Christ. It's not as though our desire to be the pietist or party animal wanes completely. But rather that each time it wells within us, we recognize it, we confess it, and we return to the love of God that remains ours in Jesus Christ. And hearing the proclamation of God's unrelenting grace sobers us up and pulls us back to the life of liberty and love that we've been called to in Jesus Christ. And indeed, the ability to come running to God—confessing each time we've obsessed over rule-keeping only to fall flat on our face or we've abused some gift of God and used it to gratify some ugly urge—is part of the freedom we enjoy. Whenever we come to God in confession, claiming Christ as our righteousness and the rationale for God's mercy toward us, he will hear us, he will speak forgiveness to us, and he will reorient us toward love. Every single time.

This is one of the many reasons why it's so critical to be part of a local church. Each week, you gather with other followers of Jesus who've made a mess of things, dabbling in pietism and being party animals. And you'll be reminded, "Oh, yeah; I'm not alone in this." And each week, together, you'll be called out of your mess and back toward the freedom found in the forgiveness of Jesus. That which the pastor proclaims to you in the service, what he teaches you in the sermon, and feeds you in the Lord's Supper, will stay with you throughout the week, rattling around in your heart. And it will become the content you comfort and commend your friends and fellow followers of Jesus with, as together you share life and seek to live out your faith in between Sunday services. A good church will be your lifeline, keeping you anchored in the forgiveness of Jesus, equipping you to engage faithfully in the questions central to a life of love, and providing you with a community of mutual account-ability and support. Simply put, you can't expect to live this life of freedom and love with any effectiveness, consistency, or joy without a connection to the local church.

Liberty and Love In Action

Some time ago, my wife and I were hanging out with our good friends, another couple we've known for years. At one point in the evening, our friend Larry[7] leaned over and asked me a question: "Would you be willing to run out and grab us a bottle of wine?" I immediately shot Larry a smile, stood from the table, and grabbed my keys. There are few things I enjoy more than a bottle of red shared with friends.

Larry asked me to get the wine because he's part of a Christian tra-dition that forbids consuming alcohol, a belief that Larry and his wife respectfully disagree with. Despite their open disagreement, Larry wasn't comfortable purchasing wine in public and running the risk of someone from his church—who didn't understand his position on the matter and with whom there wouldn't be the time, in the middle of the supermarket, to explain his purchase—to be confused or caused

---

[7] I've changed my friend's name so as to not "out" him as an occasional wine drinker. He's also a big fan of *The Real Housewives* franchise. "Larry," your secrets are safe with me.

to question his character. So, I bought it instead. As a Lutheran, no one would question me purchasing wine. In fact, they'd probably be worried that there wasn't a case of beer in my basket too.

The question of alcohol consumption offers a great test case for how a Christian, living in freedom and motivated by love, should seek to navigate life. Should you demonize the substance and outlaw its enjoyment altogether, claiming that doing so is the safest route away from sin? Or do you take a hard turn in the opposite direction, throwing even moderation and sobriety to the wind, adding a cocktail (or four) to every moment you can, all in the name of Christian liberty? The answer to both questions is no; there's a better way. Let's frame the question like this: is it possible to enjoy alcohol in a manner that demonstrates a love for God and others and that brings us—the one drinking it—joy? I believe the answer is yes.

We honor (love) God when we recognize that wine, for example, is a gift he has given to us and when we seek to enjoy it in moderation, avoiding drunkenness. The scriptures are replete with examples of alcohol being rightly and joyfully consumed. And the psalmist lists "wine that gladdens the heart of man" (Psalm 104:15) as one of many signs of God's providence. We love others (and respect ourselves) as we drink by refusing to abuse it and thereby refusing to add the complications and dangers of intoxication to our interactions. We are also loving to those around us when we are willing to abstain from drinking alcohol if, by drinking, we would create angst or cause confusion for those we are with.

To be sure, there are some activities that simply can't be rightly done in freedom and love; it's not possible to respect yourself, honor God, and serve your neighbor while doing them—for example, if an activity is illegal. Generally speaking, you can't honor God by rebelling against the authorities he's put in place. Sure, in some circumstances, offering love to your neighbor may require you to break an unjust law—see, for example, Dr. Martin Luther King's *Letters from a Birmingham Jail*. But chances are, whatever questionable activity or illegal thing you're tempted to take part in doesn't fall into the category of righteous rebellion. Likewise, there are some things that may be perfectly legal but are such an affront to God's design and intention that there's no way to redeem them, no way to take part in them in a way that isn't utterly sinful and destructive. Pornography, for example, is a horrific abuse of God's gifts of sex and sexuality. It's not possible to honor the Creator, love your partner, and bring true joy to yourself by looking at pictures of someone else's son or daughter, wife or husband, performing sex acts on your phone. Not at all.

Legality and irredeemable abuses aside, there may be some activities that simply cause you to lose control, to the point where it becomes difficult, if not impossible, for you to walk in freedom and love. You may be genetically predisposed to addiction, have a struggle with lust, or wrestle with any number of bad habits that you're prone to pursue if given the chance. Certain activities that may be perfectly appropriate for me to take part in or benign for the majority of others may trigger the worst of your impulses and therefore need to be avoided. Admittedly, doing so requires a great deal of humility and self-control, knowing where "the line" is for you and being willing to hold it, even as those around you watch the movie, sip the cocktail, or swipe the credit card without a hint of struggle.

In all of this, it's important to remember what the motivation is. We wrestle with the gifts of God we get to enjoy, the abuses we must avoid, and our weaknesses we should not indulge for a very simple reason: love. Not a love that we must earn or prove ourselves worthy of by how well we follow the rules, but a love that has already been secured for us in Jesus Christ, and we now seek to honor and celebrate in every choice that we make. It's a love that we aim to imitate, by willingly assessing our choices with the goal of showing kindness, deference, and grace to those around us. We do all of this not because we live in fear of the whistle being blown but because we know we are free, and we seek to use our freedom the way God in Christ has used his: to love someone else.

You see, the truth is that God himself has no need of our good deeds and moral behavior. Does he desire good from us? Yes. Does he *need* it from us? No. He is self-sufficient apart from our virtuous acts and without our kindness and generosity. But our neighbor is a different story. She is tossed back and forth by this crazy world. She—like you and me—is finite, weak, utterly dependent, and often anxious. It's for her that we seek to wield our liberty in love. It's for her, and for all those that we share this life with, that we seek to do our best. It's not for God; no, he's all good. But our neighbor, she's in a different boat. She needs all the good we can give.

Where the Focus Belongs

A while back Lisa and I were watching television while our youngest, Jack, slept in his nearby room. Apparently, the sound from whatever series we were streaming was a little too loud and was keeping him awake. We discovered this when, after the main character shouted something obscene, our son yelled from his room, "That's a

BAD WORD," followed immediately by the question, "Should you be watching that?!"

I headed into Jack's room, and he told me, "That's a bad show. You shouldn't watch it." Tucking him back into bed, I calmly shared that his feedback was misplaced.

"Why?" he asked. "Because I'm supposed to be sleeping?"

"No," I told him. "Because it's your mommy's show."

It's easy for us to blow the whistle. Calling fouls comes naturally to us. Even kids can do it. But the Christian faith is not, as so many would have you believe, a religious system designed to help you scratch your moralistic itch or for us to live in perpetual fear of God shaking his fist at our poor choices. Nor is it an excuse to throw away the whistle completely and abandon all restraint. The Christian faith is not about legalism or of license. It's a life of love.

It's about the love of a God who pursues and forgives us despite the harshness with which we judge each other and the abuses we allow for ourselves. He loves us so that we might know the joys of true freedom.

We are freed from obsessing over what we have done or will do wrong because all is and can be absolved in Jesus Christ.

We are freed from being enslaved to the impulse of abusing the good gifts of this world because we know that our deepest needs are met in the grace of God.

We are freed to put our focus where it belongs: on the God who loves us, the friends and family around us, and on enjoying the life we've been given.

So, may we toast with friends, laugh at good jokes, enjoy some art, and make some memories. And along the way, may we wrestle with the questions of what's right and wrong and what love requires. But may we do so with hearts unburdened from the pressure to "get it right."

When we do happen to get drunk on perfection and piety or go overboard as party animals, just call out to Christ. He won't shout judgment at us from another room—leave that to my son. No, Jesus will tell us (once again) that all is forgiven and that we have been set free.

Taking Inventory

God has made us and saved us for lives of liberty and love; lives focused on blessing the friends and family, the coworkers and neighbors that surround us. It's a better and more satisfying "why" for your life than anything offered by the items stuffed in your theological junk drawer.

And while it makes sense, odds are that as you wrestle with it you find that an important question begins to emerge. It's a question common to modern people and in particular those who are assessing their spiritual assumptions and their inherited religions. It's a question that goes something like this: "Yes, but will it make me *happy*?"

Happiness, however one decides to define it, is the highest good for many a modern man and woman. And anything that seems to impede its arrival is quickly labeled unhealthy. The pursuit of personal happiness is a dominant force in the spiritual makeup of most people. And that's why—if this process of spiritual assessment is to have integrity—we must take a hard look at the notion of happiness. Who gets to define it? Should a religion really be judged by how well it serves our pursuit of it? Is personal happiness truly the highest aim or does God have something better and more meaningful in mind?

QUESTIONS TO CONSIDER:

Which of the two extremes are you drawn toward the most? Are you tempted to be a pietist, looking to obey all of the rules; or a party animal, finding ways to bend and break them?

A life of faith in Jesus Christ is not about what we can or cannot do, but about loving God and our neighbor in all that we do. Is this a new concept for you? If so, how others-oriented have you been when making moral decisions, prior to this?

Do you feel that being "set free to focus on love" as you navigate life will add clarity or complexity to your decision making?

SEVEN

The Shallowness
of Happiness

*"The search for happiness is one of the chief
sources of unhappiness."*

—ERIC HOFFER, PHILOSOPHER

I CAN'T RECALL WHICH party it's from: the bright red coloring of the cone and the generic words, "Let's celebrate!" printed on the front tell me nothing in particular.

"Is this party hat a relic from the New Year's Eve bash we threw a few years back, the one where everyone fell asleep a good hour before Ryan Seacrest started the countdown? Or is this one of the hats I forced everyone to wear for my wife's thirty-sixth birthday party?" Because, you know, there's nothing adults love more than being forced to accessorize in front of other adults. That's especially true if said accessory is affixed to your head via a too-tight chin strap that accentuates your neck fat.

What can I say? We throw great parties. We are fun people.

The Party Hat

Stuffed in the back of your spiritual junk drawer is a party hat—the pointed, paper kind, complete with the flimsy string that no one can stand. The hat is a reminder that we love a good time. We'll go out of our way to try to fill life with as much fun as we can, even if it means looking silly in front of our peers or spending a fortune on our kids. I'm guilty of both.

It also represents a belief that many hold in regard to God. Many believe that God is a host whose highest aim is to impress his guests or that he's the parent, dying to appease his daughter as she turns double-digits. There's a belief that God exists to show us a good time and grant our wishes. We assume that if God exists and if he loves us, then—like any great host of a party or parent of a child—he simply wants to make us happy. And, after all, isn't that what we deserve?

But is that true? Is my happiness the highest aim of a good God? Or does he have something different—something *better*—in mind for us?

A New Idea

The notion of a God who exists to appease our hunger for happiness or satisfy our desires (on our terms, of course) is, in the grand scheme of things, relatively new. In the eighteenth century, a school of thought known as utilitarianism emerged. Building on earlier ideas from the likes of Epicurus, Aristotle, Augustine,[1] and Aquinas, proponents of utilitarian philosophy articulated a strict, ethical position founded upon the belief that human happiness was the ultimate good.

---

[1] Augustine famously noted, "...that all men agree in desiring the last end, which is happiness." (*On the Trinity*, Book XIII)

A utilitarian would approach everything from moral issues to the mundane demands of day-to-day life with one ultimate question in mind: "Does it make people happy?" That which produced the greatest good, for the greatest number of people, was the right thing to do.

Utilitarianism had a profound impact on western life and, in particular, the founding of the United States. One could argue that the American revolution was driven—at the very least justified—by a utilitarian philosophy. The rebellion, and subsequent independence of the colonies, were seen as morally necessary because they aimed to protect and enshrine humankind's inalienable right to "life, liberty, and the pursuit of happiness."[2] By the nineteenth century, the notion of individual happiness as the highest of ideals had taken deep root, forming a strong hold on American and European culture and thought.

This marked a significant shift. Prior to this, civil life, personal decision-making, law, and government were largely anchored in and influenced by a shared belief in universal and external truths. These were truths said to be put in place by the divine and which existed to be discerned and obeyed by humanity for our flourishing according to God's design. The question of "what is right?" was connected to another, ultimate question of "what is the will of God?" But utilitarian thinking turned the tables. Moral clarity and everyday direction were now

---

[2] Quote in context: "We hold these truths to be self-evident, that all men are created equal, that they are endowed by their Creator with certain unalienable Rights, that among these are Life, Liberty and the pursuit of Happiness." The influence of utilitarian philosophy on Jefferson, the primary author of the *Declaration of Independence*, is well documented. (Thomas Jefferson, et al., July 4, Copy of *Declaration of Independence*. -07-04, 1776. Manuscript/Mixed Material. https://www .loc.gov/item/mtjbib000159/.)

unhitched from external truths. The new thinking told us that most of the answers we sought were not to be searched for outside of man but were found within and were defined by the heart of a man. The wisdom of Sheryl Crow had begun to rule the day *long* before she penned the hook for her hit single: *"If it makes you happy, it can't be that bad."*[3]

Happy God

Our collective understanding of religion and spirituality was not untouched by this major shift toward the heart of man and the happiness of the individual. The new logic of the world quickly spilled over to our theological musings, and many spiritually minded people began thinking along these lines: "Well, if the *highest good* is the pleasure and happiness of man, then a *truly good* God must exist for my pleasure and happiness!" And let's be honest, that's a religious insight everyone can get excited about.

I have often wondered if this shift in spiritual and religious understanding helped fuel the rise of what is referred to as "the prosperity Gospel." In prosperity Christianity, the goodness of God is seen as something that largely exists to make American notions of success—a spacious, single-family home, two cars, three well-behaved children, and fit bodies that show few signs of age or illness—spring to life for the believer.

I once sat through a sermon given by the man considered to be the most famous preacher in America, a man with deep ties

---

[3] *If It Makes You Happy* is the hit single off of Sheryl Crow's eponymous sophomore album. This song, paired with *Every Day is a Winding Road* and her first hit, *All I Wanna Do*, serve as the soundtrack to roughly 97 percent of all memories from the mid 90s.

to prosperity theology. "God wants you to have the desires of your heart," he said with a smile the size of a two-door 1983 Buick LeSabre. "Do you want that new job? Do you need the nicer house? Do you want your bills to be paid and have money left over? Then just *call it in*," he urged. "Call upon the goodness of God to give you the desires of your heart." The man seated in front of me raised his hand and shouted, "Amen!" in a show of approval. Earlier in the service, my wife had noted that roughly half of the seats in the massive sports-arena-turned-auditorium were empty. Attendance was light. After the preacher's sermon had wrapped up, I pointed to a row of empty seats and whispered in her ear, "He must not have called it in." As is often the case with my attempts at humor, she was not amused.

A theology built around the notion that God's great aim is to make us happy, on our terms, has proven its ability to draw a crowd. But where it suffers is, well, in the face of suffering. What is one to make of a God who allows pain to permeate our lives, for desires to go unmet, and earthly hopes unfulfilled? A spirituality that tells you to simply "call it in" and request your own kind of hand-crafted happiness finds itself stuck when God seems to be ghosting us, leaving us "on read" or pushing us to voicemail and sending us back to our pain and problems empty-handed.

Perhaps you've personally experienced this weakness in modern spirituality. Chances are, you've found yourself in the midst of some terrible trial—miscarriage, betrayal, constant anxiety—angry at God and overflowing with questions:

"What kind of Father are you, anyway?"

"If you love me, then why am I hurting so much?"

"Don't you care about my happiness?"

"Why isn't God listening?"

If that experience and if those questions seem familiar to you, you're not alone. Many of us have learned the hard way that there is a shallowness to the notion that God exists for our happiness. It's an idea that simply can't stand under the weight, the scrutiny, the reality of the lives we are actually asked to live in God's world. There must be something more. God must have something better in mind for us than mere, earthly happiness. And he does.

The truth is that God likes it when we are happy. But happiness alone is too shallow and unsatisfying of a goal. Instead, God's plan for his people is something better: holiness.

Holiness

That word "holiness" carries a bit of baggage with it.

Many people understand that word, especially as it relates to other people, in a negative light. Holy people are self-righteous people; they act as if they're somehow better or more refined than everyone else. Imagine your little brother, now grown, coming over to enjoy dinner with you and your family. Mind you, this is the same kid who, throughout most of his life, would eat nothing but chicken nuggets and spend every spare minute playing "Army," turning everything he found into a toy gun. Imagine that this same brother shows up for dinner and announces that he no longer eats meat. "Not a problem," you think. "I can swap out the nuggets for some steamed broccoli. Yum." But it doesn't end there. He makes his announcement and then proceeds to proudly declare that being anything other than vegan—like him—is cruel and that he's "disgusted to dine in the presence of animal murderers." Your first thought would be, "Wow. Somebody thinks he's holier than everyone else." You get the idea. For many, to be holy is to be proud, arrogant, and self-righteous.

Others perceive holiness as something unattainable. "Holy" is too high of a standard for one to actually meet—with the exception, of course, of the extremely rare person who happens to embody the best of humanity. "Holy" is reserved for the likes of Mother Teresa,[4] who dedicated her entire life to the poor, and for Betty White[5] whose joy and comedic genius endured for nearly a century and made her something of a secular saint. Holiness, in the minds of many, is something out of reach for the average person, reserved instead for compassionate nuns and *Golden Girls*.

In the Christian faith, to be "holy" simply means "to be set apart." Specifically, it means to be marked and set aside for service to God. The apostle Peter, in the New Testament letter that bears his name, uses the Greek word, *hagios*—translated to English as "holy"—to describe the Christian church. He writes:

---

[4] In 2007, some of Mother Teresa's personal and private correspondence was published, revealing that the saint's own spirit was often in anguish, struggling for a half-decade with a sense of God's absence; proving that even the "holiest" among us are not immune from spiritual anguish. Teresa's struggle should not shake less publicly pious believers, but rather comfort them. We all face difficulties, spiritual and otherwise. And there is no lasting peace to be found even through the most profound acts of service and love on our part, but only through the sacrifice and love of Jesus, who is stronger than us all, even Mother Teresa.

[5] Seriously, White was around longer than the Hollywood sign itself (1922), endearing herself to multiple generations, cementing herself as an entertainment icon, and doing it all without a hint of scandal. If Betty ain't holy—in a secular sense—then who is?

But you are a chosen race, a royal priesthood, **a holy nation**, a people for his own possession, that you may proclaim the excellencies of him who called you out of darkness into his marvelous light. (1 Peter 2:9 - emphasis added)

According to Peter, the church is a collection of holy people, but this holiness has nothing to do with us being exceptionally moral or righteously picky about our food. It's not about some level of perfection the church has attained or an attitude of superiority we've adopted. No, the holiness spoken of in the Christian faith describes the fact that the baptized, the believing, have been chosen by God *despite* our immorality and our unrefined sensibilities. In our baptisms God established in us a dependence upon the person and work of Jesus Christ, a relationship of utter reliance upon *his* perfection, *his* faithfulness, *his* sacrifice for our sins, and *his* rise from our grave. And this faith, this dependence and reliance, makes the church distinct and set apart. There is a whole new theme and focus in the lives of the forgiven. Before, your life may have been dominated by some other idea, such as success in your field, shame carried from sin, political passions, or sexual orientation. All of that has been supplanted by something better. Your life no longer exists for you, but to love and serve this person, Jesus, upon whom you're fully dependent. You are set apart. You are holy.

Identity

I share this with you, realizing that it might set off an alarm in your brain. It's an alarm that typically sounds like this: "Run! He's got the wrong person. My life is too much of a mess to be lived for Jesus. I've done some shady stuff. I'm *doing* some shady stuff. How could I be set apart for Jesus? Doesn't he deserve fine china? I'm more like a paper plate." Sound familiar?

But this is where the beauty of the Christian faith really shines. Holiness is more than a new calling upon your life. It's a new identity in the eyes of God. When you were baptized into God's family and you received saving faith in Jesus Christ, a great exchange[6] took place. You received all that Jesus Christ possesses to keep as your own. And Christ received, in exchange, all that you possess to keep as his own. You received his perfection, his right relationship and preferred status[7] with God the Father. It's yours. Likewise, Jesus took all your issues with him to the cross as his own. He died for them, earning forgiveness for it all, and rose from them, breaking their power over your life. All that's good about Jesus is now yours. All that's bad about you belongs to and has been conquered by him. And now, when the Father looks at you, he doesn't see you; at least not the same you that YOU see. He's cleared out your history. He's closed all the tabs of the terrible things you've said, done, and struggle with to this day. And

---

[6] The notion of a "great exchange" comes to us from Martin Luther: "Accordingly the believing soul can boast of and glory in whatever Christ has as though it were its own, and whatever the soul has Christ claims as his own. Let us compare these and we shall see inestimable benefits. Christ is full of grace, life, and salvation. The soul is full of sins, death, and damnation. Now let faith come between them and sins, death, and damnation will be Christ's, while grace, life, and salvation will be the soul's; for if Christ is a bridegroom, he must take upon himself the things which are his bride's and bestow upon her the things that are his. If he gives her his body and very self, how shall he not give her all that is his? And if he takes the body of the bride, how shall he not take all that is hers?" (*On The Freedom of a Christian*, 1520)

[7] "...behold a voice from heaven said, 'This is my beloved Son, with whom I am well pleased.'" (Matthew 3:17)

now, when the Father pulls up your name, all it shows is Jesus Christ. You have a new identity.

Now listen, I get it. You don't *feel* all that holy. You can't look at your life and see any empirical evidence of your becoming some kind of new creation in the eyes of God through faith in Jesus Christ. Sure, God calls you holy, but you still look and feel...regular. That's normal.

I remember when my wife and I signed our then five-year-old son up to play baseball. We paid the registration fee and were emailed a list of the entire team roster. Jack Popovits was listed along with a dozen other kindergarten students. He was on the team. With the registration came a jersey and hat, which Jack was very excited about and quickly put on, running around the house screaming with excitement about baseball. My fatherly heart was overflowing with pride. "My son is a ballplayer." And of course, before the first practice I made sure to deck him out with every imaginable accessory and piece of equipment: baseball pants and belt, cleats, gloves, bats—all of it. I didn't want him to be unprepared. What if this tee ball thing really took off? He could go pro.

Jack showed up to his first practice fully equipped to play the game. He was on the team, he had the uniform, and his dad had decked him out with every essential resource. I sat behind the backstop and watched him and his fellow five-year-olds try to make sense of their coach's commands. I watched as my son grabbed the ball tossed to him by the coach and, rather than toss it back, decided to indulge in a game of keep-away. That is until he plopped down on the grass and said, "Okay. I'm done! It's over, right?" As the practice wrapped up, the coach gathered the kids together. He gave them a short pep talk, but it was clear the kids weren't listening. It didn't matter. In reality, he was trying to communicate a message to me and the other parents: "Don't get upset that there's a lot to learn," he said. "That's what this season is about. We are learning to play the game."

That moment stuck with me. And, quite honestly, it was a bit of a relief to me. My son had the role and the resources to play the game, but he didn't have the skills. At all. But it wasn't as though I'd failed him as a parent. No, he was right where he was supposed to be. That age and stage of the game is not about crushing it but learning and growing into it. The same is true in the Christian faith. We are made holy. We are set apart and given a brand-new identity through faith in Christ. We have the roster spot, the uniform, and all of the resources we'll need for this new calling. But just as it was with Jack, the goal of the game is not to crush it. We can't. So, take some pressure off yourself. The goal is to learn and grow into who you are. The apostle Paul, in his letter to the Philippian church, put it like this:

> Therefore, my beloved … work out your own salvation with fear and trembling, for it is God who works in you, both to will and to work for his good pleasure. (Philippians 2:12-13)

God has accomplished our salvation and applied it to us. He's made us holy. He has, in Paul's parlance worked salvation *into* us. The task of the Christian is, over the course of his or her life and with the non-stop empowering of the Holy Spirit, to work this new identity *out of* us, allowing its implications to take root in our lives and shape who we are. It's a life of learning, *as* a holy people, how to *be* holy people.

Purpose in Pain

The implications of this realization—that God has gifted holiness to us and is working holiness through us—cannot be overstated. It's a truth that, as you lay hold of it, begins to fill your life with meaning and purpose.

We'll start by looking at how it transforms our understanding of pain. Consider this: if God's great goal for your life is holiness then purpose can be found, or forged, in every single difficulty you face.

If God exists to simply make you happy, according to however you or the culture define it, then every struggle, every pain and problem you encounter, is a betrayal. He's letting you down. And then, there is no way to reconcile the tragedies that occur and the mistakes you make. Picture yourself running a marathon. If life is purely about happiness, then God's job is to give you water and cheer you on as you dash toward your desired goals. And every heartache is him sticking out his leg to trip you up. But take note of how the Book of Hebrews speaks of our struggles:

> God is treating you as sons. For what son is there whom his father does not discipline? If you are left without discipline, in which all have participated, then you are illegitimate children and not sons. Besides this, we have had earthly fathers who disciplined us and we respected them. Shall we not much more be subject to the Father of spirits and live? For they disciplined us for a short time as it seemed best to them, but he disciplines us for our good, that we may share his holiness. (Hebrews 12:7-10)

The writer of Hebrews invites us to remember that this is our Father. And what do good dads do? They don't just throw parties or stand along the sidelines of life, holding up signs and cheering you on. A good dad will confront you about hard things. He will correct you. Sometimes, he will even step back and allow you to struggle. Why? Because a good dad has a greater purpose in mind. He knows that his job is not to indulge his child but to mold and shape the heart and the character of his child. And to help facilitate a larger, long-term plan of flourishing.

At your baptism God chose you; he made you his own and marked you as his child. You're beloved by him; you belong to him and have been set apart for a life of growing into his love for you. Your suffering is not a betrayal or a stumbling block. Your pain can now be seen as part of his plans. This is not to say that he plans bad things to happen to us, but rather that he uses all things for his larger purpose in our lives. When bad things happen, you can say, "God is doing something. He is up to something. My life exists within his story and is being guided by his loving, fatherly hands. What's happening now—though I don't like it—has purpose."

Reflect for a moment. What's your biggest struggle in life right now? It could be something massive, or it might be something small. Whatever it is, picture it. With that image in mind, say these words to yourself: "God is not letting me down. God is working for my good." It takes faith to say it, doesn't it? And yet, that's God's promise to us. He uses our struggles to build character, shape our hearts, foster things like patience, or deepen our trust in him. He could even be using this struggle and how you face it as an instrument for his own glory. As you hold to him and trust in him in the midst of trouble, you are bearing witness to a weary world that our God is good and worthy of praise.

Deep Dependence

Have you ever noticed how, sometimes, when a person gets everything they want, they become the worst possible version of themselves? The celebrity who lets success go to her head and is suddenly too good for the people and places she used to know prior to fame? Or what about the working-class couple who finally hits it rich playing the lottery, only to have the money disappear and their marriage fall apart due to some bad decision-making? Sometimes, when we get what we want, we can't handle it. It handles us.

The social sciences talk about something called the hedonic tread-mill.[8] It's the tendency in humans to return to a baseline of happiness (or unhappiness) despite positive events or life changes. For example, you get a substantial raise at work, or you finally go on that long-awaited vacation. And while there was much anticipation in the run-up and incredible enjoyment in the moment, the buzz wears off with surprising quickness. Despite now being better paid and well rested, your mental and emotional state adapts and returns to where it was before. We think success leads to lasting happiness. But both our experience and science tell us otherwise.

If anything, one could argue that we are more of a danger to ourselves on the mountaintops of life than in the valleys. Success, however we find it, usually ends up making us hungrier, not happier, striving for that elusive high. It creates a pressure to hold on to it and an appetite to experience even more of it. And it also has a

---

[8] Social scientists Philip Brickman and Donald T. Campbell invented the term in a 1971 essay entitled, "Hedonic Relativism and Planning the Good Society." Since then, much has been written about the hedonic treadmill and a quick online search will reveal many helpful summaries and explanations.

way of inflating our sense of self and loosening our grip on God. My guess is that it's quite rare for people, when they are at the height of success, to feel as though their relationship with God is thriving. Human nature is such that when I'm doing poorly I blame God, and when I'm doing great, I forget him.

In contrast, when holiness is the goal it has a way of renovating the heart and reorienting one's focus. When you understand that God has gifted holiness *to* you and is working holiness *in* you, you are driven away from a life of self-obsession and self-reliance and toward deep dependence upon Christ. A life that's about growing in service, trust, and gratitude toward God in times of joy and pain is a life where you will feel—keenly—your need for Jesus. Specifically, you'll find yourself clinging to him as your example and your assurance. Let's look again at Hebrews:

> ...let us run with endurance the race that is set before us, looking to Jesus, the founder and perfecter of our faith, who for the joy that was set before him endured the cross, despising the shame, and is seated at the right hand of the throne of God. Consider him who endured from sinners such hostility against himself, so that you may not grow weary or fainthearted. (Hebrews 12:1-3)

I have a few friends who are serious runners. One of them likes to compete in ultra-marathons. Apparently, 26.2 miles is too easy. He prefers races thirty, fifty, or seventy miles in length. He's crazy. At this moment, I don't even have enough gas in my car to drive that far, let alone the energy or ability to *run* that far. But my friend is different. He told me that the key to a really long race is to have another runner in mind whom you admire and who can inspire you as you run—someone whose example you can focus on for guidance and whose faithfulness to the race can inspire you to endurance. The writer of Hebrews is telling us that Jesus is the hero upon whom we set our eyes as we run this race. We fix our eyes on him, the perfect example of the holy life. His obedience, in the most difficult of all situations, inspires us and guides us. We look to him for motivation to live a life for the Father's glory and not merely our own ease and happiness.

More importantly, along the way, we are driven to Christ for assurance. As the race gets difficult, it's normal for us to question our standing with God. It's normal to wonder whether or not he's mad at you or if the problems you're facing are him punishing you. Perhaps you're wrestling with such questions right now. If so, I encourage you to lift the eyes of the heart and mind to the cross of Jesus Christ. This is our assurance of God's attitude toward us. Yes, God the Father hates your sin—more than you can imagine. But he loves you so much that he took his hatred of your sin and placed it fully upon his son, Jesus Christ, instead. He was punished once and for all, including for you. The Father is no longer in the punishment business; it was all dealt with and done in Christ. Yes, life is hard. But rest assured: it is not punishment; you are loved.

Likewise, as we seek to live out and grow into the holiness that has been wrapped around us through faith in Jesus Christ, we are drawn to continually depend on him as a source of grace. There are moments every day where it becomes obvious that we are horrible at being holy. We're horrible at trusting God, horrible at loving our neighbors, horrible at even remembering God. So often we fly through our day without so much as a thought of him, living as practical atheists.

I'll say it again: we are really bad at being good. And yet, there is a constant stream of grace flowing from the cross of Jesus Christ toward you and me. Every time we realize our failures, each time we are confronted with the cold, hard truth of our cold, hard hearts, the Holy Spirit draws our eyes back to the sacrifice of Jesus. Staring at that cross, we hear the words, "Christ has died for this. You are forgiven for this." Over and over, we cling to those words as if our lives depend on them. And indeed, they do.

More Beauty

But there's more. A life of holiness not only gives us purpose in our pain and fosters deeper dependence upon Jesus, but it brings beauty into our broken world.

Adding beauty to this world is not something that comes naturally to us. Things like love, sacrifice, generosity, and patience are not natural occurrences in a world where so many feel entitled to their own personal definitions of happiness. Birthday-party-style happiness lives and dies on the idea of getting what you want. But truly beautiful things call us to do what's required and to give—typically to others—not what we *want* but what is *needed*. And this has to be taught. We need to be trained.

Just take a good, long look at the small children in your life. Yes, they're cute and wonderful in so many ways. But they are also thieves. All of them. Natural-born burglars. The easiest word for them to learn, other than "mom" or "dad," is "mine." They toddle around your house, grabbing your keys, drinking from your cup, opening your drawers, all while endlessly mumbling, "mine … mine … mine." I once watched a toddler grab a cookie off a table and stuff it in his diaper.

Thieves. Adorable thieves. It's the default setting as humans. And it won't change unless a parent steps in and teaches them something better, something that adds beauty to our world, such as how to ask by saying "please" or how to share something with others.

And the same dynamic is at work between us and God. We are born into his family and made holy in his sight through belief and baptism. And then he invites us to live a more beautiful life than we would otherwise pursue on our own. He calls us out of stuffing cookies down our pants and into something better. He will ask you to forgive your sister-in-law rather than hold on to your hurt like a prized possession. He will call you to give what you'd rather keep to someone in need. He will urge you to confess your issues to him and stop kidding yourself about the severity of your sins. He will push you to commit to the woman you've been dating rather than to keep stringing her along. He will convince you that you need to stop flirting with that coworker and to instead stay focused on your spouse. He will nudge you to pursue peace with your enemy. He will call on you to pray for the coworker who speaks poorly of you behind your back. None of it will be easy. None of it will instantly fill you with feelings of happiness. All of it will cost you something you'd rather hold on to, something you might even feel entitled to.

The counter-instinctual things that God calls us to do bring glory to his name and add a small speck of beauty to our world. And they also serve to train us, little by little, in the things of God. Again from the writer of Hebrews:

> ... all discipline seems painful rather than pleasant, but later it yields the peaceful fruit of righteousness to those who have been trained by it. (Hebrews 12:10)

God guides us to do things, to make choices that go against our broken instincts, but which are a blessing to this world. He guides us to choices that train and transform us, choices that—to us—can feel like death. (Let's be honest: who, at first, truly *wants* to forgive their toxic coworker or enjoys letting go of their hard-earned money to someone in need? Anyone?) But to God, these difficult choices are nothing less than beautiful fruit. They are the beautiful fruit of his own Holy Spirit at work in us, of the holiness of Jesus that he's given to us.

Perhaps there's a choice right now that is staring you in the face, and the right thing, the holy thing, is clearly marked for you. But you've been avoiding it because it will cause some discomfort. It will cost you something you crave. It will get in the way of some other immediate gratification. If life is about short-term, shallow happiness, then you should continue to avoid what you know to be right. But what if all that we've said up to this point is true? What if God has called you, saved you for bigger and more beautiful things than self-gratification? What if it's true that God put you here for more than grasping at everything you want? What if he's trying to train you, to bear some fruit, and to add some light to this darkness through you? Then it will require that you refuse the impulse to just "do you." Instead, you'll need to embrace the holy thing, the hard thing. You must choose to do the right and beautiful thing. Today.

Higher Hopes

My two children share the same birthday month. One year, to save on cost and to make it easier for the friends and family who'd want to celebrate, we combined their respective celebrations into one big party. I soon discovered that coming up with a theme that would please two very different children, separated in age by nine years, would not be easy. My effort to bring their parties together under a theme of "things that their father loves," such as '80s pop-culture, obscure and out-of-print theology books, and fine-tasting yet affordable Scotch whisky, proved neither successful nor appropriate. We went with "circus." Not all that original, but nonetheless a hit. The petting zoo put it over the top.

Truth be told, their mother and I were determined to plan a party that our kids would truly love. We wanted to make a memory. For us, it's part of being a good parent. It's also what birthday parties are for: feeling like the center of the Universe and getting what you wish for. Plus, if you have to share it with a sibling, it might as well be worth it. Cue the petting zoo, pony rides, and all-you-can-eat candy buffet. We went all out. Although, a whisky-themed party would have been fun. Just saying.

Day-to-day parenting, however, is different from party planning. Every other day, my concern as a parent is not what my kids are wishing for but who my children are becoming. I'm less concerned with making a memory and more focused on making them into a certain kind of human being. These children have been entrusted to us not to indulge their desires but to mold them into people who bring honor to our family name, glory to our God, and who add beauty to this difficult world. We want them to grow up and to someday move out of our home, holding an unshakeable peace, paired with an ever-present joy. And we won't get there through parties alone. We'd be negligent as parents. We have higher hopes for them than a surface-level happiness.

And God, your father, has greater hopes for you too.

Not Bad, Just Not Best

Please understand: happiness is not a bad thing. God loves to see you smile. It's just not the only thing. Do you know what's better than happiness? Joy. And perhaps that's what we've been after in this chapter. Joy, a deep-seated contentment and sense of wellbeing, is what we really want. And joy is the byproduct of pursuing and embracing something bigger, deeper, and richer than happiness itself. It flows from knowing and resting in the love that God has for you and walking the path that he's set aside for you. Joy is a fruit of holiness. It comes from abiding in the truth that God sees you and accepts you as good, through the work of Jesus Christ. And that he's set you apart for a life of leaning upon his love and following where he leads. It comes from holding tight to promises like these:

> He is making you into someone new.
> There's purpose now, even in your pain.
> You're part of his plans which, though daunting, drive you to Christ.
> He's making the world a more beautiful place through you.

We want a life of party hats. But there's a shallowness to mere happiness. Thankfully, God knows better than we do. And he is up to something so much greater.

Taking Inventory

Thus far we've sorted through some significant items, addressing some of the most critical (and common) spiritual misconceptions. And as we turn toward the close of our spiritual spring cleaning what remains is another foundational piece, a cornerstone of warped religiosity. It's our unrelenting desire for control.

The Christian faith teaches that a primary struggle in the heart of every human is the desire we have to do God's job, to take his title and to grab the steering wheel of our lives. In our hunger for control, we elevate and obsess over (you could say we worship) all kinds of things, thinking they can make us sovereign over our circumstances. We are determined to be the masters of our own fate, subject to no one. Not even God.

I call it a desire for control. Historically Christians have had another term for it. They simply call it idolatry.

QUESTIONS TO CONSIDER:

Do you feel pressure to find and maintain a certain level of happiness in life? If so, where do you believe the pressure is coming from? Is it an instinctual urge, or is it fueled by outside forces, such as the stories told on social media or the manufactured discontent of modern marketing?

Do you struggle to believe that there can be purpose in pain? Can you think of any good things in your life that have been borne out of incredible difficulty? If so, what are they?

How does the idea of holiness as a higher goal than happiness make you feel? Do you have any concern that, should your focus shift to higher aims, you'll somehow miss out?

EIGHT

The Centrality
of Idolatry

"I'm not superstitious but I am a little stitious."

—MICHAEL SCOTT, THE OFFICE

LISA AND I HAVE been married for more than twenty years. Early on, I learned a valuable lesson, one that has helped ensure the health of our relationship and the happiness of our home. The lesson is this: the thing you're fighting about is *rarely* what the fight is actually about.

This breakthrough came from a pair of socks—my socks—that I had left in the middle of the living room. To call it a living room is generous; it was more like a "living corner" in the 550-square-foot apartment that we rented as newlyweds. My nightly habit, one that far pre-dated our very young marriage, was to lounge on the couch, take in a television show, and, at some point, pull off my socks and drop them on the floor next to me. I had no idea what happened to the socks after that point. In my years prior to marriage, they would magically disappear from the living room floor, clearing the way for me to drop another pair in their place the following night.

Lisa would have none of this. For a few weeks, she tolerated the sock dropping until finally, one morning, she came to me with tears in her eyes and my crumpled socks in her hands. There was also an anger in her voice that, to that point, I'd never encountered. We dove into a heated discussion—others might call it a flat-out fight—about how our tiny living room is not my personal clothes hamper. I countered that it was just two socks: not that big of a deal. To which Lisa responded, "Treating me like a maid is a big deal!" The rest is a blur, but I remember at least one sock flying at my head and the door to our bedroom being slammed shut. It was then that a fresh insight flashed in my brain: "I don't think this is about socks."

It wasn't about socks; it was about the disrespect that Lisa felt in my assumption that she would pick up after me. It was about the worries she had of being seen as "Mother 2.0" to a husband who'd grown up in a home where crumpled socks, dirty dishes, and unmade beds took care of themselves. It was about the hurt she felt as I disregarded her multiple pleas to help keep our tiny apartment free from clutter. The thing we were fighting about wasn't what the fight was actually about. Thankfully, slammed doors reopened shortly thereafter, and Lisa and I were able to have a meaningful conversation about what lay beneath the surface of our spat over socks. And I'm happy to report that, after twenty years of marriage, my socks are rarely found on the living room floor. And, if they are, they are taken to the hamper shortly thereafter by my own hand.

This simple lesson is an important one, not merely for marriage but also for faith. Behind all of the ways in which we get faith backward or turn our understanding of God inside out and upside down stands a larger reality. There's a more foundational problem. The things we discuss on the surface are just the tip of the proverbial iceberg. If we hope to truly make headway in our effort to rightly understand the Christian faith, then we need to take a deep breath and dive beneath the waves. We need to examine the real issue beneath all our spiritual struggles.

The Rabbit's Foot

Some say its origin is in Celtic Britain, around AD 500. The left hind foot of a rabbit, captured in a cemetery during a particular phase of the moon, was said to hold certain properties and powers. Snag that foot and carry it with you, and the arc of all things would bend in your favor. With that hind leg in your possession, you could call yourself lucky.

Whatever the origin—and there are many and varying legends—you've got one: a lucky rabbit's foot. There was a brief moment in the late 1980s (or was it the early 1990s?) where they were in fashion, or at least relatively common. The lucky rabbit's foot was the kind of thing you'd get as a prize at the carnival for popping a balloon with a dart. It was cheap and fake (few actual rabbits were harmed by this trend) and dyed an obnoxious color so as to stand out. It was designed to be used as a keychain. But being twelve years old at the time you acquired it, you had no keys to chain. So, instead, the severed thumper bounced up and down on your backpack, swinging from its zipper throughout most of middle school. And for some reason that you can't quite explain, you still have it.

It's buried in the corner of your spiritual junk drawer. Finding it, you pull it out and examine it. "How in the world do I still have this thing?" You're tempted to drop it in the trash. But you pause. Something in you doesn't sit well with tossing it out. "What if throwing it away brings some bad voodoo?" you wonder. "I mean, it *has* managed to stay with me all these years." You roll it around in your hand and feel its fading nylon fur. Staring at it for a few more seconds, you drop it back in its hiding place, purposely burying it under a few other items. "Silly little thing," you think. "I really should throw it away." But instead, you leave it buried. "Who doesn't need a little luck?" you mumble to yourself. And with a bump of your hip, the drawer is closed.

The rabbit's foot is not about superstition; it's about something stronger, something bigger. Within each of us is a desire to ascribe deep, divine power to the silliest of items and ideas. We take what are—in the grand scheme of life—trifles and turn them into talismans, carrying them with us and insisting they will bless us. It's a very bad, very strange, and (spiritually speaking) very deadly habit. We assign powers to pieces of creation that actually belong to the Creator. We seek from the earth that which can only be found in God. It's not superstition; it's deeper. It's idolatry. And it is the root of the tree, the heart of the matter, the underside of the iceberg. Idolatry is the thing behind all the other things.

One Commandment

The Christian faith talks a lot about sin, the catch-all term for the innumerable ways in which we live outside of God's good and perfect will. Our sins are many, but humanity's central, spiritual struggle is with idolatry. It's the first of the Ten Commandments: "You shall have no other gods before me" (Exodus 20:3). And it's been said that if we could just get that first one right, we'd have no need for the other nine.

Why is it that we take things that don't belong to us? Why do we struggle to respect those in authority? Why do we ruin marriages with infidelity and so glibly defame the names of others? Why do we murder? Why is it that we can never, ever be content with what we have? Is it a case of simply having not read the commands of God close enough? There are many reasons we give for the awful things we do. But they are, in the end, just symptoms and not the disease itself.

The truth is that we sin because there is something we long to possess or protect to feel whole. It could be an object, a person, or a certain idea. Whatever it is, we run to it for refuge, we trust in it completely, and we afford it our faith. And as a result, we are able to justify any action in order to attain it, rationalize any activity in order to protect it. There are things more important to us than God himself. And so, we don't bat an eye at breaking his commands in order to serve them.

The apostle John authored three short letters that are found near the end of the New Testament. The first of the three ends with what some might read as a non-sequitur. After pointing his hearers toward faith in Jesus Christ, his final line is simply: "Little children, keep yourselves from idols" (1 John 5:21). The letter itself is about love. It is a beautiful call to faith in Christ, who is the love of God made flesh, and for us to love for one another as his forgiven followers. Why, then, this abrupt ending on the subject of idolatry?

For John, love and idolatry are connected. Idolatry is what happens when our love is confused. God's love is to be our greatest love. But in our sinfulness, we subjugate what God the Father has done for us in Jesus Christ to second-tier status. By closing with a commendation to steer clear of idols, John is telling his hearers—and us—to keep what we adore in check. We are to let the love of God in Christ Jesus (so beautifully articulated in his letter) be the top hope in our hearts, the ultimate object of our faith, the great treasure we hold dear. When God's love (Christ) is our true love, it flows downhill into every other aspect of life, infusing our daily existence with things like kindness, peace, and patience—the fruit of his influence. But when our love gets turned around, idols are what emerge, which then give way to all manner of delusion and dysfunction, leading down a road of self-destruction.

Little ones, steer clear of idols.

Bad Exchange

The apostle Paul, in his letter to early Christians in ancient Rome, offers a succinct description of idolatry, albeit without actually using the word. In chapter 1, Paul describes the many ways in which humanity—deluded, dysfunctional, and destroying itself—was living out of step with God's design. It's a very specific list. Paul had taken good notes. And no doubt much of what he described was not just taking place "out there" in unbelieving Rome but could have been found within the community of Christians on the receiving end of his letter. Indeed, it's impossible for anyone—present company included—to read the last half of chapter 1 and not feel called out. Ancient or modern, author or reader, we are all a mess.

Just prior to his convicting list, Paul offers a rationale for our behavior. He tells his audience why things have devolved into their crazy, corrupted state. Yes, it comes down to idolatry. But listen to how he describes it: "They exchanged the truth of God for a lie, and worshiped and served created things rather than the Creator" (Romans 1:25). It's all the fruit of a bad exchange, a terrible trade. We've swapped the truth for lies. Specifically, we have exchanged the Creator for creation. *That* is idolatry at its core. It is believing the lie that a created thing is your god or that a created thing can give you more of God.

Notice that there are two aspects. In the first, we are committing idolatry by functionally replacing God, acting as though some object, idea, or person is ultimate and seeking from that thing the blessings and benefits that can only come from him. Think back to the Old Testament story of the golden calf. God's people have escaped slavery in Egypt. Moses, their leader, has ascended to the top of Mt. Sinai to receive instruction from God. But the people get restless. Moses is taking too long with the Ten Commandments. In their impatience, they gather up their jewelry, melt it down, and make a metal cow. They call it god and plan a feast to celebrate its arrival. And then— worst of all—they take the credit that God deserves for their escape from slavery, and they pile it onto this DIY deity, saying, "You're the one who sets us free." Their story may seem silly, but more than anything, it should sound familiar. Is it really all that different from putting your career, your kids, your possessions, or the acclaim of your peers on a pedestal and then living as if they're ultimate? And why do you do it? It's not simply because you love these things; it's because, in your heart, you—like the impatient Israelites—have bought into the idea that by offering your all to these created things, you'll no longer have to wait on God. You can sacrifice to these statues, enjoy your freedom, and get on with life. The real God can seem so far away, like he's stuck on a mountain with Moses. So, you replace him. You believe they can offer you the same blessings and benefits: lasting peace, wholeness as a human being, or validation that can erase your guilt and silence your shame.

The other side of the idolatry coin is believing that, by giving your utmost attention to some element of everyday life, you can manipulate God or get more of him. It's the idea that, if you excel at some task or acquire certain things, then God is duty bound to bless you. It's a video game approach to God. Gather the right items, finish a few side quests, and you'll "level up" in his eyes, receiving more resources, gaining access to greater powers, and displaying more strength. Religious people are particularly prone to this kind of idolatry. "If we say the right prayers at the right times, or if we give a little more money to our church or show that we are truly generous to the plight of the poor, or if we are disciplined in our habit of daily devotions, or if we vote for the right leaders, then Jesus *must* respond in kind by blessing us." It's idolatry, but not the cow-making kind. We are worshiping the false god of our own effort, believing the true God is beholden to our religious activities.

Whether you're seeking something from creation that can only come from the Creator or you're seeing your own performance as a creature as a means to manipulate the Creator, it's all the same sin according to Paul. You've grabbed hold of something smaller than God, wrongly believing that if you squeeze it tightly or serve it rightly, it will force his hand or replace him altogether.

You've swapped the truth for a lie. And lies lead to dysfunction.

Digging Deep

If you find yourself thinking, "Do I have any idols in my life?" you're asking the wrong question. It's not a matter of if you've got some idolatry going on but where idolatry is present in your life. Idols are like crazy uncles—we all have at least one; or, in my case, three. If you're not sure where your idolatries lay, I encourage you to reflect on three areas of life that serve as decent indicators of when and how creation has trumped the Creator. Consider the obsessions of your mind, the spending of your money, and the triggers of your emotion.

Let's start with the mind. William Temple, the Anglican priest and former Archbishop of Canterbury, once wrote, "Your religion is what you do with your solitude."[1] Where do your thoughts immediately go when other things are not commanding your attention? Do you find yourself constantly pondering other people's opinions of you? In the back of your mind, are you constantly crafting your rise to influence and acclaim in your field? Is it sex? Is it a search for affection and acceptance in the arms of others? Perhaps it's the condemning voice of a person from your past? To what does your mind snap back when the distractions of the day fade away?

Consider your finances. Jesus famously said, "Where your treasure is, there your heart will be also" (Matthew 6:21). If you'd like to know where someone's hope is anchored, you can learn a lot by examining where they put their resources. Is there an area of life in which you are continually overextended financially? Is there a certain item or

---

[1] This quote is attributed to Sir William Temple (1628-1699), and it is a convicting notion. Does anyone love God so much that he alone dominates their solitude? Likely not. But the point is nonetheless well made; where our hearts and minds wander reveal our true desires and deepest devotions which, so often, are far from the Divine.

indulgence² that you can throw cash at with ease, to the frustration of family or friends who see it as a waste? Or is it that you refuse to spend and rarely share, saving—stockpiling—every cent you can? Why? Because seeing a bigger and bigger number each time you pull out your phone and check your balance fills you with peace beyond comparison.

And then there are your emotions. What triggers your moments of greatest joy? What drags you into a massive funk, in an instant and without fail? These triggers are telltale clues of where our worship is going. Do you really love the sweet moments with the kids? Is it the meaningful exchange with your toddler that brings you joy, or is it the sense of superiority you feel about being an engaged and intentional parent that warms your heart? And why is it that a sudden change of plans stirs up such intense anger and annoyance in you? Is it really because the person canceling is being inconsiderate? Or could it be that such abrupt edits to the calendar offend your need to feel in control? Last-second changes disrupt the illusion of a perfectly ordered world, which you idolize.

It's not fun to reflect on these things. But it is important. Think of it like gardening: it's tempting to just examine the surface of the plant, to look at the leaves for any signs of trouble. But any good gardener will tell you that, from time to time, you need to put your hands in the soil and see what you find. You need to pull back the

---

² I'll go first: it takes hardly any effort at all to convince myself that I need a new pair of sneakers or the latest iPhone. And I am well aware of the psychology behind it: having new shoes and the latest technology make me feel, at least for a second, like an accomplished and successful person. For a few days, the creaseless sneakers and the smudge-free phone help quiet my insecurities.

dirt. All kinds of pests can live beneath the surface, attacking the root and killing your hopes for a harvest of homegrown tomatoes. It's the same for us as spiritual creatures. Now and then, it's good to get our hands dirty, to dig deep and see what's stirring beneath your actions and assumptions, what's feeding the choices we make, the money we spend, and the emotions we feel. When you expose the root, you'll often find some annoying idol holding on tight, chomping away and looking to ruin your harvest from the inside out.

Idolatry Unchecked

Right about now, you might be thinking, "Okay, but so what?" Perhaps you follow all of my logic thus far. You agree that we tend to worship things that aren't God trying to get gifts that can only come from him. And you nod your head in agreement at the notion of humankind using things in our world as a means of influencing the Divine, thinking we can get more of his blessings through our own performance.

It all makes sense. But still, you think, "So what?" Why is it important for us to recognize the lucky rabbit's foot buried in our spiritual junk drawers? I mean, if you're not a Christian, you likely don't feel beholden to God's command to avoid idolatry. And if you are a Christian, then you believe that the grace and mercy of Jesus Christ, won for you on the cross, covers over your idolatry. So, what's the point of stirring all of this up? A lot could be said as to why this is a worthwhile conversation, Christian or not. And yes, at the top of the list is this: idolatry is an offense to the one true God, which should be reason enough to make people of faith eager to expose their functional saviors. But consider also the effect your idolatry has on you and those around you.

Idolatry, unchecked, is enslaving and destructive. It often leads to the suppression of your personal freedom and to the harm of people you care about. These small, created things that we bow down to eventually loom over us and become sources of anxiety and pain. Consider, for example, the way many of us approach our careers. We throw ourselves into work, thinking that we will find acceptance, affirmation, and all that we need to be a whole and happy human being by accumulating more and more vocational success. It becomes an idol. But what you discover is that, with your career as an idol, every setback or frustration you experience on the job balloons into something bigger. It's no longer just a problem at work; it's a hit to your heart, an attack on your joy. Work problems become existential threats. But it gets worse. Even your good days, your 'wins' at work, are cause for more anxiety. Successes are short-lived. Just as you prove yourself on one project, you'll need to start from scratch and prove your worth once again. You never actually arrive. Coworkers are no longer seen as human beings with whom you can share meaningful moments and a significant portion of your life. You don't get to have friends at work; you have competition. You have obstacles and adversaries on your way to salvation—to wholeness, happiness, and enoughness[3]—via marketplace success and an ever-increasing salary. Not only that, but you lose control of your emotional well-being. The approval of your boss, the advancement of other colleagues, gain a stranglehold on how you think and what you're feeling at any given moment. In short, the whole scheme backfires. The career that you've

---

[3] "Enoughness" is a word first defined and best used in David Zahl's profound book, *Seculosity*.

idolized, that you've worshiped as a way to attain freedom and joy, robs you of it.

The things that we worship end up harming us and others by crushing us under the weight of the expectations we heap upon them. Consider the pressure we put on relationships to make us happy and whole. If what you love, more than anything, is the applause and approval of others, then you are in for a rough road. What you'll discover is that there is always another person to impress, another crowd to convince. There will always be someone in the corner, arms crossed, who is not buying what you're selling. The unending service you must provide to the god of affirmation, by way of constantly proving yourself, will eventually wear you down. Or think about the individual people we so easily idolize. We build pedestals in our minds and place our spouses, our kids, our bosses upon them. We believe that they are, in some way, the crucial element in our thriving and joy. The better they are at their vocations relative to us, the happier we will be. We do this without truly wrestling with what we are demanding of this other person. We are insisting that someone else help make us whole. And they won't be able to do it. But since our own well-being is on the line, we will continue to demand and desire the impossible. And all the while, we'll tell ourselves that we are loving them. But idolatry is not love. When we idolize others, we are setting them up for failure. And failure in the face of impossible expectations is fertile ground for resentment to grow and bitterness to burn.

The ancient theologian, Augustine of Hippo, wrote in his Confessions, "[Lord] You have made us for yourself, and our hearts are restless until they find their rest in you."[4] There is a satisfaction, a wholeness, a peace that can only come from God. When we hold lesser things in our hands, demanding they give us that which can only flow from the hand of the divine, we will never have enough. And if we persist, we may just grasp it so tight that we harm both the thing we hold and ourselves in the process. This is why the scriptures use such forceful language, imploring us to "put [our idolatry] to death." Doing so honors God, and it protects us.

Emptying our Hands

All that said, the instruction often given by well-intentioned Christian leaders at this point is not helpful. It boils down to a call to recognize the rabbit feet found in your drawer, gather them up, throw them away, and just do your best to love God more. The advice of most preachers—on this and just about every other issue—is "cut out the bad stuff and try harder at the good stuff," which, as you might guess, turns out to be completely unhelpful and ineffective.

I live in Texas—the southeast corner of the state, to be exact. And when we purchased our first home, we quickly noticed that we had a bug problem. We had a cockroach issue. And by issue, I mean dozens of roaches, most the size of a small car, crawling throughout our home. After our initial panic, we called an exterminator who treated our home, sending each one of our roaches to their final resting place. As he was about to leave, I thanked him and naively stated, "I'm glad

---

[4] "Thou has formed us for Thyself, and our hearts are restless till they find rest in Thee." (*Confessions*, i. 1)

we will never have to do this again." He smiled at me and said, "Son, you live in Texas. The bugs are big and bad. They dip tobacco, drive a truck, and never give up a fight. They'll be back. And so will I." With that, he handed me his card and walked out the door. He was right; the roaches returned. It's just part of life in southeast Texas. Some things, like the roaches in Houston, never go away. You don't solve the problem; you learn how to manage it. And in this case, you come to the realization that you'll befriend the bug guy. Every three months, he knocks on my door. He's a more frequent visitor than most of my friends and family.

This side of eternity, we will not fix our idolatry issue—at least, not completely. It's not something that we can simply stop, no matter what some preacher shouts at you. The roaches return. Rather, we must find a means of managing it so that we are not overrun by it. This happens by first ridding our minds of the notion that we will cure ourselves of anything or fix ourselves at all. The way to deal with our idolatry has little to do with our own efforts. The antidote to our idolatry comes from the outside in. It's not cured by us. Instead, it is dealt with through a rhythm of confession and forgiveness, a lifestyle of regularly admitting idolatries to God and resting in the promise of forgiveness and mercy he hands us in return. We'll take a deeper look at this in the next chapter.

For now, let's look again at the words of 1 John:

And we know that the Son of God has come and has given us understanding, so that we may know him who is true; and we are in him who is true, in his Son Jesus Christ. He is the true God and eternal life. Little children, keep yourselves from idols. (1 John 5:20-21)

Before telling us that we must flee from our idolatries, John reminds us of what we have in Jesus Christ. John declares to us that we are "in him" and that he is true, that Christ is not a false God but the real God. For John, fleeing from idols begins and ends by returning to—and resting in—that which we already possess in Jesus Christ, namely the forgiveness of sins. We keep ourselves from idols not in the sense that we run from them in fear but by emptying our hands. We drop them to the ground and discard them for the powerless trinkets they are when compared to Christ. We can't help but release the idols from *our* hands each time we are re-awakened to the good news of Jesus and all that awaits us in *his*.

Jesus Is Better

And in case you're wondering, in case it's not quite clear, Jesus is, without question and beyond any doubt, better than any trinket we are tempted to worship. Can he handle your hopes and dreams? Can he give you the meaning, the assurance, and the love that you long for?

The answer is yes because of what history and the Christian scriptures tell us he did for us in his death and resurrection. In his death, Christ took upon himself the just punishment of all of our sin, the payment necessary for our endless idolatries, and all the dysfunction they've wrought. And then he rose from the dead. He came back to life and walked out of the grave victorious, proving that his death satisfied the demands of justice and that all of his promises were trustworthy and true. He died and came back to life like he'd told the world he would. And so, Jesus gets the benefit of the doubt on every other claim that he made: like that he is God's own son, even God in the flesh, that life without end and immeasurable mercy are found in him, and that he's capable of carrying each one of our God-sized needs on his resurrected shoulders.

The Christian life is a life of realizing (often the hard way) that you've been loving something the wrong way, asking too much of it, and ascribing too much power and priority to it. It's a life of recognizing that you're clenching some kind of "lucky rabbit's foot," dropping it to the ground and then returning to the person and the work of Jesus. And each time you come back to Christ, he doesn't lord it over you—though he is the Lord. He doesn't say, "I told you to cut this out" and demand you demonstrate your devotion. He simply says what John repeated throughout his letter: that he loves you. False gods will always ask for more from you, always demand more of you. But Jesus, the true God, couldn't be more different. He doesn't say, "Do more." He says, "I am enough. My cross forgives you. My empty tomb assures you. My grace is sufficient for you." And that, my friends, is so much better.

Very Superstitious

I've never been much for superstition—I don't carry any trinkets in my pockets, I don't have a pair of lucky socks, and I have zero anxiety about stepping on a crack or walking under ladders. I did, however, have a lucky rabbit's foot when I was a kid. I'm fairly certain it wasn't real. I doubt that the Chuck E. Cheese, where I acquired it in exchange for 200 tickets at a fourth-grade birthday party, cared much for quality and authenticity in its prizes. I lost it as quickly as I got it.

But, as we've learned, I'm prone to ascribing otherworldly power to and placing divine expectations upon the toys and trinkets of this world. And so are you. In that sense, we are all superstitious. We are all holding tightly to earthly things that are incapable of meeting our deepest needs. And that's the issue beneath all the other issues. We are trying to wring meaning, peace, and satisfaction out of creation rather than leaning upon the Creator.

Let us not give ourselves over to or relegate our lives to it. Let's admit it. Let's confess it. Let us run regularly to the truth that there is a real God worthy of our love, capable of delivering on all our deepest needs, and able to shoulder our divine expectations. He is a God overflowing with mercy for those who mix up and misplace their devotion. His name is Jesus.

And he doesn't have any luck to offer you.

He's got something better: undeserved and unending love.

Taking Inventory

With that, we've completed the process of critiquing and culling our spiritual assumptions. And as it stands right now, your junk drawer may look as though Marie Kondo has had her way with it. It's probably pretty bare.

But we are not done just yet. There are a few final, and important, questions for us to consider. Where do we go from here? Now that our collection has been cleared, now that our junk drawer is empty, what are we to do with it? And is it possible to keep from filling it right back up with backward, broken, and burdensome junk?

QUESTIONS TO CONSIDER:

Idolatry is a hard and heavy word to contemplate. Do you agree with the assertion that your life is laden with things competing for your ultimate allegiance? Why or why not?

Consider again the quote from William Temple, "Your religion is what you do with your solitude." Where do your thoughts go when nothing else is commanding your attention? What might this tell you about the idols that exist in your life?

Idolatry is about control. The idol is a means to lay hold of God's authority and to get what we want. In which area of life is it most difficult for you to relinquish control to God and to trust in his power and his plans?

NINE

Continued Curation

"Truth, like gold, is to be obtained not by its growth,
but by washing away from it all that is not gold."

—LEO TOLSTOY

LISA AND I HAVE made several cross-country moves. We've packed up everything to make a home in Texas and then left Texas to spend several years in New York City, only to come back to the Lone Star State. And prior to all that, we bounced around the Midwest, moving from Michigan to Missouri.

With each cross-country move, Lisa and I have made a promise to each other. After long hours of packing things into boxes, giving items away to friends, and stacking what's left in the driveway to sell to neighbors, we are spent by the process. And disappointed in ourselves. We wonder how we've accumulated so many things that we care so little about. And then we make a vow. It goes something like this: "In this new house, it won't happen again. We will let go of non-essentials, and we will not accumulate so much stuff. We are starting over. From here on out, we will keep closets and drawers, the attic, the garage, whatever storage space we are blessed to have as empty as possible."

But inevitably for us, once we land in our new place, every square inch begins to be occupied. And before we know it, despite promises made and best intentions, our house is again filled. Even for a family like ours that seeks to live somewhat modestly and minimalistic compared to most, it is alarming how quickly we re-stock our lives with inconsequential items.

What we are learning, as obvious as it sounds, is that it's best not to wait until the week of a move to start sorting your things and deciding what matters. It's best to do so as part of the rhythm of day-to-day life. Yes, it will make things easier when it's time to pack up and head to a new home. But more than that, the occasionally curated closet and drawer, attics, and garages can dramatically improve the quality of life in your current home.

Continued Curation

Spiritual junk drawers, like our homes, don't stay empty for long. Despite whatever promises we've made and our best intentions, we will find more religious assumptions, moralistic memes, and spiritual half-truths to keep, even if, as you've read these pages, you've come to see that the person and work of Jesus is the only thing that you need. You'll be alarmed at how quickly our spiritual lives become cluttered with conflicting, confusing, and generally unhelpful items.

Much has been said and written in recent years about deconstruction among people of faith. It refers to the process by which some—typically those steeped in American evangelicalism—question the theological foundations they've been handed and seek to remove or reject that which no longer feels authentic to themselves and true to the world as they now know it. While others may say the opposite, this author doesn't believe the process of deconstructing one's faith to be inherently bad or spiritually dangerous. Quite the opposite. I think that, when done fairly, it's a healthy, even explicitly biblical, pursuit. After all, what was Jesus doing throughout the gospels but dismantling the sacred spiritual assumptions of his contemporaries? He rooted out falsehoods, named idolatries, and invited (in some cases demanded) his listeners to leave them behind. But here's the key: he always replaced it with something truer and better. Namely, himself.

In some sense, deconstruction is what we've been undertaking throughout this book. We've been looking at the spiritual assumptions we carry, poking holes, and pulling at threads, seeing if they come apart at the seams. And when they do, you've been invited to replace it with something better, with something true. You've been invited to replace it with Jesus—not with a particular theological tradition or a specific denomination, just Jesus. But like the items we so quickly collect in our brand-new home, other assumptions will take the place of the ones you've pulled apart. Other ideas will find their way into your metaphorical junk drawer. As such, this deconstruction, this intentional curation, needs to continue. We should not wait until the end, whenever and whatever that is, to clear out this clutter. It must become part of the rhythm of our everyday, spiritual lives. We should regularly assess the ideas we accumulate, take a critical eye to the assumptions we carry, and compare it all to the message of the unmerited mercy won for you in Jesus Christ.

Repentance

Repentance. It's a loaded and painfully theological word. It's not one that you're likely to throw around in everyday conversation. Start using "repent" with your coworkers or your kids, and you'll start getting sideways glances from your own flesh and blood and an invitation to meet with HR the next time you're in the office: "We're told you've been making your teammates uncomfortable."

It's a loaded word, for sure, but a good one, nonetheless. It's especially helpful as we consider what an ongoing life of spiritual curation looks like on a very practical level.

The word repentance was most famously used by John the Baptist, cousin and forerunner of Jesus sent to "prepare the way of the Lord." John called those within earshot of his voice to admit their need for God, to set aside any pretense of spiritual self-sufficiency, confess their sins, and, in doing so, ready themselves to reorient everything around the Christ—the Savior—to come. And once he arrived, Jesus picked up the same message: "The time is fulfilled, and the kingdom of God is at hand; *repent* and believe in the gospel" (Mark 1:15, emphasis added). The act of repentance—no matter what images come to mind for you, no matter the baggage you carry associated with the word—means being readied to believe, to be reoriented around good news.

Fast-forward some 1500 years and Martin Luther is preparing his *95 Theses* to nail on the door of the Wittenberg Church in Germany. These ninety-five theses are a series of propositions for a theological debate Luther would like to have with the Catholic Church. In Luther's mind, the church was making it difficult—if not impossible—for people to hear and receive the message of salvation by grace through faith alone, apart from any kind of moral striving. These ninety-five theses would be the match lighting the fire of the Reformation and would, no hyperbole, change the world.

The very first of Luther's theses read like this: "When our Lord and Master Jesus Christ said, 'Repent' (Matthew 4:17), he willed the entire life of believers to be one of repentance."[1] Don't miss what Luther asserts: it is the desire of Jesus that, for those who follow him, their entire lives be ones of repentance.

Our entire lives. Repentance.

Again, if we understand repentance only in terms of angst-filled, guilt-ridden confessions of terrible wrongs, watery eyes, and heaving chests proclaiming that we will never, ever do that bad thing again, then Luther is painting a dark and depressing view of Christian life. Indeed, conviction, confession, and contrition over sin are all aspects of repentance. But they're not the whole of it. For a fuller picture, we pivot to the one who made it famous. We look to John the Baptist. Repentance is, above all, being readied for Jesus. It is turning toward him and away from lesser things. This is what I believe Luther had in mind with the first of his world-changing 95 Theses. The Christian life is one of continually turning toward Jesus—in big things and small things, on Sundays while in church and on Thursdays during your ride home from work, recognizing the goodness of God in Jesus Christ compared to whatever else you'd done or indulged in earlier that day.

Think of repentance as the original act of deconstruction, only it's not focused externally, on the theological foundations of your

---

[1] Martin Luther's *Ninety-Five Theses Against Indulgences* (1517).

particular church body, but internally. It's self-critique. Martin Luther's preferred translation of *metanoia*—the Greek word typically rendered as repent—was "come to your senses" or to "wake up and change your mind." In that sense, repentance is enlightenment. It's honest, personal reflection upon your actions, the story that you're telling yourself on repeat in your mind to make sense of the world, and the other religious assumptions you've stuffed in your back pocket, and asking yourself, in reference to all of it, "Is this better than Jesus?"

Is this better than a savior who lives, dies, and rises for me and then asks for nothing in exchange for all that he's done for me?

Is this better than the promise that I am already right with God and guaranteed a glorious and peace-filled future, apart from any moral donation on my part?

Is this better than life without end in a re-created and perfectly whole world, ensured not by the earnestness of my belief or my contributions to society but by the fact of Easter morning?

Is a God who tells me to come to him when I'm weary and find rest for my soul better than a world that relentlessly encourages me to keep my head up, hustle, and to reach my full potential?

The answer, of course, is yes, to every question, every time, every day. Jesus is better.

Repentance is nothing more than admitting that whatever you've been engaged in, wrestling with, or holding on to for some sense of peace, purpose, sense-making, or salvation pales in comparison to Jesus. It's embracing, celebrating, and returning to the supremacy of grace given in Jesus over and over again. It's returning in big ways and small ways, in the occasional, dramatic tear-filled confession and in the more numerous and mundane moments of simple recognition and redirection.

And as this repentance becomes part of the rhythm of your life, your spiritual junk drawer can't help but be continually curated. With your heart regularly redirected toward Jesus, you'll regularly sort its contents, comparing it to Christ. You'll keep what drives you to lean on him more, and you'll toss that which clouds the comfort of knowing "it is finished" (John 19:30).

An Awfully Good Church

The other important factor in nurturing your faith is to be part of a local church. As mentioned in earlier chapters, spirituality is considered by many to be an entirely private affair, a personal matter. We are hesitant to express it in any kind of corporate way. But such an attitude is a threat to a healthy reliance upon Jesus.

One's faith is meant to be made stronger by being in close proximity to others who are holding tight to the same truths. It's designed to be fed by gifts that can't be experienced by listening to a preacher on a podcast, reflecting on some devotional sent to your inbox, or by watching a church service online streamed to your phone. Like the tiny packet of fruit snacks I toss to my kid in the middle of a long road trip, such things can only tide you over for so long. They can't satisfy your deepest hunger. At some point you'll need to stop for proper sustenance.

And I get it; most churches are kind of awful. If you're not part of one, it's likely for a reason. And it's not a superficial one, like having to roll out of bed early on a Sunday morning or the unwelcoming aesthetics. Although, as an aside, most churches are doing themselves no favors when it comes to basic hospitality. Between the lack of signage to show a guest where to go, the absence of anyone to greet you and make you feel welcome, the weak coffee, and the musty smell filling the air, it's as if they're daring visitors to bail early and head to brunch. No, the biggest issue of all, the reason so many stay away, is because of the people.

Churches are filled with profoundly imperfect, downright dysfunctional people. And they're not just filling the pews. They're preaching the sermons and playing the music. Gathered within those church walls are people likely to annoy you, discourage you, perhaps even hurt and disappoint you.

The people. That's what makes church seem so awful.

But please hear this: it's also what makes being a part of one so essential.

The truth is that you're kind of awful too. It's been said that if you're not the worst sinner you know, then you don't know yourself very well. And what sinners need is to be part of a community where we can freely admit our faults and where we can be reminded—week after week—that we are not alone. The church was never meant to be a collection of good people getting better but a community of train wrecks receiving triage. Church is meant to be a place where the facade of our abilities and awesomeness can be safely set aside, and we can dare to admit that we are no better, no less broken, no more spiritually capable than the highly paid executive seated next to us or the girl who's all of five seconds sober and barely hanging on slinking into the pew in front of us. Church is supposed to be the place where the faith we have in ourselves comes to die, and we are safe, by virtue of the messy people *around* us, to admit the mountain of mess that exists *within* us.

The mark of a good church is not how put together the people are who call it home, but how honest they are about their dysfunctions and the emphasis placed on Jesus as the source of their comfort and strength as sin-sick people. Yes, you need a good church. You need it so that you can receive the comfort that comes from being welcomed into a fellowship of the broken. And you need it because it is the place where God has promised to show up.

Indeed, that's the primary task of the church—to give you Jesus. When the preacher offers a sermon pointing you to the cross, that's the church giving you Jesus. When the elderly member of the congregation gets wind of a difficulty you're experiencing and promises to pray for you, telling you to "take heart because Christ is in control," that's the church giving you Jesus. When the pastor stands in front of the small crowd on Sunday and announces your sins are forgiven or hands you bread and wine and says, "take and eat," it is the church giving you Jesus. Sure, it's all wrapped in weakness and at times a bit awkward and weird. But this side of eternity, that's precisely where God has promised to be found. What else would you expect from a God who won the war with sin and death by losing his own life on a cross? By being found in and among the mess that is the church, God has positioned himself on the bottom shelf, so to speak. He's accessible to all people, especially the awful ones. He's completely within our humble grasp.

Quite often, I'll be asked to offer recommendations to churches. Someone's niece will be moving to an unfamiliar part of the country, and her Uncle Bill will shoot me an email asking if I know of any "good churches" in that area. They assume that as part of seminary education, pastors are made to memorize the address and Google reviews for every church in the nation.

Rather than give a recommendation, I tend to offer up three questions. These questions are helpful in finding a church to which you can truly belong, continually grow, and stay oriented around Jesus.

First, ask "*Is it local?*"

Is the church you're considering close enough for you to be involved beyond Sunday morning? Is there a high likelihood that the people you'll meet as you exit a worship service are actually your neighbors? If your goal is to have a supportive and life-giving community to be a part of and to be committed to for more than just a few months, then attending a church that's truly local is critical.

Second, ask "*Is it invitational?*"

Does the church have a posture of openness and warmth for those outside of her walls? Do they hold events or offer ministries that meet a need for those who are not a part of the church? Do they greet you and make you feel at home when you visit, and do they attempt to make the service, regardless of style, understandable to any newcomers? Or is it a cold community with a foreign culture that outsiders are left to learn and adapt to on their own?

Third, ask "*Is it Christocentric?*"

Is the church focused on the person and work of Jesus Christ as the foundation upon which everything is built? When a church is living out the historic faith, rooted in the scriptures, the heart of that community will be to know and love Jesus more and more.

A quick way to try and discern if a church is Christocentric is to analyze the grammar. As you sing the songs and as you listen to the pastor speak, who's getting the attention? Who is the hero? Specifically, who is the subject of the sentences? Who is the "doer" of the verbs? If every song is, "*I* want to" and "*I* need to," and every sermon is about "what *you've* got to do" and "who *we* can become," then that church isn't all that Christocentric. They aren't attempting to give you much Jesus. They're just offering advice. And let's be honest, if advice is all you're looking for, there are easier ways to find it than rolling out of bed at seven on a Sunday morning.

A Greater Affection

You could make the case that this book has not been about metaphorical junk drawers or the deconstruction of our modern, western idolatries, but about love—or its close cousin, affection. As detailed in the previous chapter, we have wandering and promiscuous hearts. Aware that something is wrong within us and around us, we cast affections on any number of things that might help us make sense of it all, that could quiet the confusion or offer us some sense of control. As such, the primary aim of this book has not been to merely illuminate the many faults and failures in the spiritual items we hoard. If that's all that was accomplished, then we've accomplished very little. The goal has not been to show you the flaws in your many affections, but to show you a greater Love altogether.

This language comes from Thomas Chalmers, a Scottish minister and Christian leader in the early nineteenth century. In his most famous lecture, Chalmers argues that it is pointless to deal with mankind's struggle with sin and our endless idolatries by illustrating how bad such things are, by threatening the pains of hell, or by exhorting people with a loud voice and a wagging finger to just "cut it out!" Even if you were successful at getting them to drop their current obsession, they'll just replace it with another.

The only effective way forward, Chalmers argues, is to illustrate that God in Christ is better and more beautiful than any other attachment, that he is supremely worthy of our heart's attention and devotion. He asserts that there is an "expulsive power" to a new affection. In other words, once Christ, with all that he is and all that he's done, is proclaimed to a human heart, it cannot help but purge itself of lesser loves. "The root power of sin," Chalmers says, "is severed by the power of a superior pleasure—a more compelling joy."[2] And once this joy is discovered, the wellspring of which is Jesus, it will reign supreme. Sure, on this side of eternity, broken hearts will continue to entertain other suitors, but in the long term they will find that there is no comparison to Christ.

My goal has been to show you the beauty and the supremacy of Jesus and to awaken a greater affection. We have rummaged through your collection of spiritual ideas, grabbed a few of the most potent and stood them side-by-side with his cross, his empty tomb, and the ridiculous yet wonderful promises he's made.

I'm hopeful that your heart is stirred.

I'm praying you've discovered, or have been drawn back to, a superior pleasure, a more compelling joy.

I'm holding out that through a rhythm of repentance, led by God's Spirit, and by belonging to a local church that continually gives you Christ, your curation will continue. You'll keep sorting through

[2] Thomas Chalmers, *The Expulsive Power of a New Affection* (Wheaton, Illinois: Crossway, 2020).

spiritual items and competing allegiances with a critical eye. And that you'll remain anchored to Jesus, running to and resting in, the work that he's done.

Worth His While

I'll offer you one final compelling look at Jesus. Take it and tuck it away in your spiritual junk drawer, give it a place of prominence in that closet we've just cleaned out. I'd love nothing more than for you to stumble upon this truth down the road, perhaps in a season of struggle when you're scouring your various hiding places for some semblance of hope.

Here it is: Jesus suffered the worst and found it worth his while.

That phrase comes from the writing of Dorothy Sayers, one of the most insightful writers and theologians of the twentieth century. It's found in her essay *The Greatest Drama Ever Staged*. In it, Sayers expounds on the lengths to which God has gone, in Jesus Christ, to demonstrate his love for us:

> The incarnation means that for whatever reason God chose to let us fall ... to suffer, to be subject to sorrows and death—he has nonetheless had the honesty and the courage to take his own medicine. He can exact nothing from man that he has not exacted from himself. He himself has gone through the whole of human experience, from the trivial irritations of family life and the cramping restrictions of hard work and lack of money to the worst horrors of pain and humiliation, defeat, despair, and death. He was born in poverty and suffered infinite pain— all for us—and thought it well worth his while.[3]

---

[3] Dorothy L Sayers, *The Greatest Drama Ever Staged* (London: St. Hugh's Press, 1950).

Christ has endured the worst that human life has to offer out of love for humanity, out of love for you. Any pain you experience and any hardship you endure, Jesus has been there. He has shared in the struggle. And it wasn't a chore to do so, some terrible obligation he felt compelled to fulfill, rolling his eyes as he took on flesh and joined our world. No, taking on our burdens was his joy.

Has anyone ever loved you like this? Have any other so-called saviors—the centers of other sense-making philosophies, the stars of other peace-promising ideologies—done anything even remotely comparable for you? And even if they had, don't you think that they would then ask for something in return from you, that they would leverage their sacrifice for some massive measure of devotion? But what ask has Christ made in return for his life and death? None. What admission price does he demand for you to enjoy the fruit of his work? Nothing.

He chose to experience your pains, to die your death, and to rise from your grave because of what it would accomplish for you, not because of anything he could get in return from you.

It was simply worth his while.

You, messy and imperfect, were well worth his while.

You, forgiven and free, were well worth his while.

Take that truth and affix it to the inside of your drawer. Give it some permanence and prominence in that place where you stow away spiritual notions. And every time you pull it open to drop some other junk in, may it remind you—may it declare to you—that Jesus is better.

In him you already possess all that you will ever need.

QUESTIONS TO CONSIDER:

Take some time and flip through the preceding chapters, reacquainting yourself with the spiritual assumptions that have been addressed. Which of the seven metaphors resonated most deeply with you, and why? Can you articulate how this assumption has changed, or how it was challenged, when compared to the person, work, and promises of Christ?

How does a rhythm of repentance, as proposed in this chapter, make you feel? Does the routine curation of your spiritual assumptions and a regular reorientation to Jesus sound difficult and depressing, or does it strike you as an invitation to spiritual rest and relief?

Are you a part of a local Christian congregation? If not, what has kept you from attending and being committed to one? If you are, do you find that it's easy to take part or are there forces—personal and/or cultural—that hinder more regular participation? If so, what are they?

Reflect for a moment on the many descriptions of Jesus, and what he's done for you, offered in the preceding chapters. Of the things you've read about him, what stirs the most affection?

Acknowledgements

WRITING THIS BOOK WOULD not have been possible without the generosity of my family, especially my wife and best friend, Lisa. Thank you for affording me the time to put down these words. I know it came at the expense of time spent with you. I love you.

I'd also like to thank the people of St. Mark Houston who I am so blessed to serve. The trust that you extend to me as your shepherd and the freedom you offer to focus on projects such as this one are treasures that I do not take for granted.

Thanks also to Chip May and the team at Camp Arcadia in Arcadia, Michigan. It's my favorite place in the world. This book wouldn't have gotten off the ground without that week spent on the shore of Lake Michigan, closer to God than one can otherwise get.

Thank you to Rachel, the best teammate a guy like me could ask for. The encouragement and accountability you provide is just what I need.

The same goes for the crew at 1517 for their profound patience and their gentle nudges to cross the finish line. I'm particularly grateful for Dr. Jeffrey Mallinson. His insights, critique, and consultation proved invaluable.

Thank you to Kristina Deusch, for not only lending your editorial help and expertise to the manuscript, but for encouraging me to get started in the first place.

ACKNOWLEDGEMENTS

To Matt and Shannon Engelman and Steve and Sheree Martin, your generosity and constant encouragement are a gift from God.

I also owe a debt to my friend Frank Hart of Atomic Opera, whose song "Jesus Junk" served as inspiration for the title, and, in some ways, the very mission of this book.

And lastly, to the many people who have come to me with questions and who have given me the high honor of helping them sort through their spiritual issues and assumptions over the years. This book was written with you in mind. Every time I sat down to write I imagined you sitting across from me. Thank you for the companionship and the inspiration.

Index

Scripture Index

About the Author

MATT POPOVITS WAS BORN in Flint, Michigan but now lives and works in Houston, Texas where he serves as Senior Pastor of St. Mark Houston, a Lutheran church and school. Previously, Matt served as Pastor of Our Saviour New York (OSNY) in New York City.

Matt is the host of *What Matters Most* radio and co-host of the popular podcast, *Make It Simple.* He's also the author of *Tough Call: A Little Book on Making Big Decisions* and is a regular speaker at events and conferences around the world.

Matt is married to his high school sweetheart, Lisa, and is the proud dad to Ava and Jack.

For more information: mattpopovits.com

Find free companion
Bible study materials
& sermon notes for

JUNK DRAWER JESUS

at 1517.org/**junkdrawerjesus**

More Best Sellers from

FIFTEEN · SEVENTEEN PUBLISHING

1517.

Find these titles
and more at 1517.org/**shop**